Contents

Chapter 1

Everyday Landlord

Read this first or risk forever being lost.

This book chronicles our long landlord life. This is not a house flipping book, it is not an advice book. It's a Landlording book. My stated goal in writing it is to 1st make some book sales thereby giving me validation as a writer. 2nd to share our experiences and help other people. It is most certainly not to tell you what to do. My hope is that readers will benefit from our experience and then forge their own future.

I have strong opinions formed by thirty plus years of living the life. We started out young and naïve, became older and wiser. We scratched, sweated and did what had to be done every day. We raised our children in and around rental homes. Surprisingly, or not, most are heading down their own landlord path.

Our experiences are not typical, my choices were not always best, it is what it is. We recognize what we have done and accomplished is an anomaly in a world of conforming expert opinion.

Now, beyond retirement age, but not drawing SS, we are still landlords, we struggle with easing out of the business we created. We are selling, leasing and trusting properties. As of this writing in 2018, we hold title to eleven homes, some free and clear, some with small debt. I am truly grateful that for much of our career and all of the last decade we have been completely supported by our tenants paying rent. This book tells how we did it.

How to use this book

Read it cover to cover or go back to the contents and select a title. It does not matter. This book was written with the express purpose to help people landlord and learn from our experience. Every one of us is a little different and we know where we are headed better than anyone. Don't follow our path or any path blindly, gather information where you can, process it with what you know and take your best shot. But take aim first.

Later, bask in your successes, spend your profits, and keep learning. There is no such thing as a free education in landlording. What you do affects your outcome for better or not. Make smart choices and your education will be paid for many times over.

In the beginning

Boy - where do I start? How do I start? I want to help you by sharing our landlord experiences, but I am not telling you what to do. You know your own big picture better than any author and you make your own decisions. The fact that you are reading books on landlording makes me wonder if the prior statement holds *water. I guess I can start by apologizing for offending you., That backhanded comment was not called for but was intended to get you thinking. Sometimes I poke at people, and this book is full of pokes and prods, it's my way. But not to be mean, to be your friend. I really do enjoy helping others, and I believe you should do the same, please pass it on.*

> *This book is not like any other, I relate*
> *thirty years of real landlord life.*
> *renting - buying - selling - getting out*
> *It's up to you, to take away*
> *what you can use.*

Now, on with *Everyday Landlording*

Linda and I met in 1976, on our first date I talked about property, sailing, and water well drilling. She probably talked some too. I remember us excitedly discussing classified newspaper ads stating - $100 down / $100 month - $250 down / $250 month to buy houses. Wow, terms were cheaper in the 70's, but not that cheap. I called the person running the ads and got the lowdown, he was an attorney. Even back then at my tender young age, I knew that was a red flag. He was renting houses on lease options. I guess he or his clients owned or controlled them. Anyway, after talking at length on the phone, I declined to have any more contact and walked away. Why? Simple, I didn't like him, not what he said, it was how he said it. My gut feeling was to run far away from him before I regretted something.

A business born of necessity.

Our first rental arrived like our first child - no one knew for sure when it would arrive or what to make of it when it did. Linda and I ultimately had seven children and twenty five or so rentals. Or was it the other way around? After a stint as a railroader, wholesaler and unfulfilled builder, I decided to put my varied skills to use as a handyman. I remember my very first job offer, a fellah asked if I would rake leaves. It was two days before Thanksgiving and he was getting his yard in order. It felt like a gut punch when he said rake leaves. I felt weak in the stomach while he waited on the line for my answer. I thought how drunks hit rock bottom, was raking leaves my rock bottom or is porta-potty pumper next? I said, "Sure, I'll rake leaves, I want $12/hr and I would start in the morning."

Fast forward.

I have done hundreds of handyman jobs, I raked that fellahs leaves for three more years. Our company was called *Skilled Handyman Inc.* We specialized in rental repair and employed our guys full time. Linda headed up the home front, ferried kids and kept me grounded.

My guys worked on our own rental property as much as on our customers.

Sam's House

I am meeting my customer at his late father's empty house. Sam has flown up from his home in California to close his dads estate. Sam had hired me over the phone to paint and install wood shutters on the homes two front windows. I think I bid $50 plus the shutters and one can of spray paint.

The work took under thirty minutes, so we talked. He was going to list the house for sale hoping to wrap it up and get back to his home and wife asap.

I know you see where this is going. We settled on $42,500 with a $2,500 down payment. I don't remember the exact interest rate or payment, but it was around 10% apr over twenty years.

We did not have all the down payment, I told Sam up front I would have it in two months, but in the meantime, if he agreed, he could go home knowing the estate was taken care of. He said maybe - but he had to meet Linda first. We arranged to have coffee the next morning. We brought two babies and had to be back by noon to pick up the three and four year old at preschool.

Sam must have liked the kids and Linda, we shook on the deal and concluded the paperwork long distance.

I can only surmise that Sam trusted us and got the deal he wanted. I believe mostly he wanted to finish up his fathers estate and go home to his wife. We wanted our first rental at a fair price and terms we could handle. It was a win win. We both went away happy. One could say we were lucky, but it wasn't luck at all. We were in the market looking for a deal and we were prepared to move on it when an opportunity presented itself. ***That's not luck, it's being prepared.***

Sam's deal for him was not much cash but ***huge piece of mind. We gave him a promise he could trust.*** Obviously he gave us our first rental house. He did not do us a favor or help us out anymore than we did him. In a way we both traded for something we wanted and money was only a small part of what it took to make a deal.

We will talk more about Sam's house later in the book. Meanwhile, the last two paragraphs hold two secrets and are worth rereading.

> *Landlording has not consumed us, on the contrary, it has afforded us time to put family first and make a decent living while building wealth.*

Great deals are created

You have probably heard a comical variation of the *Golden Rule* that goes something like, "He who has the gold, rules." While that is essentially true in many situations, it is not at all my interpretation. In my way of thinking money is only a small part of what all of us do in business and our lives. I think all deals, all interactions may be broken down into bare requirements and needs. But since we always attach a money value to everything, we often find ourselves unable to put together simple deals where both parties come away happy. Barter is common place in parts of the world and in our pioneer days was the only means of getting anything accomplished. A man with a goat would trade it for a bushel of wheat. That is the simplified ideal deal. Both parties get what they want.

In buying and selling real estate I have learned to try to identify the sellers and buyers true wants. Of course, everyone says money but I have proved to myself multiple times that there are other more motivating factors at work. If you look beyond the dollar signs, *trade equally, fairly, and* understand that the true desire is not always money. If you do this, and are prepared when opportunity knocks, you will end up with all the property you want. It seems funny when I think back but we became over worked and had to stop looking at houses in order to slow down and stop acquiring them. Too much of a good thing I guess.

I repeat, *look for what they want, not what are they asking.* It is a minor difference worth noting and is the essence of making deals where everyone wins. This one action on my part has been responsible for many of our purchases with little to no money up front.

Consider this: An older couple is selling their beach house, they say they hate to sell but are tired of all the work, driving back and forth, and fixing things. You guessed it, for this couple it is not just money, it is freedom to not have to work and be responsible for their beach house. So why not offer them continued limited use of the house, but you immediately take over maintenance and in return they give you an option or contract with favorable terms. Perhaps with zero

16

down payment. It has happened this way for us several times, not beach homes but homes where the owner does not need a down payment. Instead they need relief.

Another example: The long time property owner states she has turned down developers offering to buy her last small forested acreage where she grew up. She also mentions she does not want the trees cut. Her true value is the living trees, and her childhood memories, she is ready to accept an offer that preserves what she wants. It is not always the money. (The property where we currently live and built our family home is the basis for the last example.)

Now that we have gone almost full circle in over thirty years, we are cutting back our landlording, we have made deals selling our rentals where we have not required large down payments. We wanted out of landlord management, not a bag of cash. It's absolutely true, discover what they truly want and then address it in your offer. The money will somehow work out, it always does, you will see if you look.

> *Being landlords has been our ticket, but I know it is not for everyone. I have always (almost) been able to do what I want and I enjoy my work, not everyone is so lucky.*

First Education

I purchased my first house in 1974. It was a late 1880's fixer without a functioning heating system. My payments were $78/mo on a contract sale. I was twenty three and had a good paying railroad job but then I was laid off for seven months. "Welcome to the real world John!"

When I bought the house, certain things came together. First was my unknown to me at the time, rule about trading fairly. I didn't recognize my own success formula for twenty five years. Never the less I employed it, I made a deal for $78/mo agreeing to fix up the house, starting with a furnace and roof. The previous owner must have noticed I walked the talk (had a job) another rule, so he trusted me to do what I said I would do. Lastly, we both trusted our gut, a method experts warn to avoid. Trusting my gut feelings has served me well so far, I'm sticking with what works for me.

> *This book is about being an everyday landlord,*
> *that means it's ultimately all about money.*

Choosing Associates

Good luck. More than once I have complained to Linda that I can't accomplish anything or get anything done. I will go down my current list of calls I am waiting to be returned and then follow it with my complaints about not being able to hire people except unemployed ner do wells. One day I came home complaining that I couldn't get the guy on the corner holding the sign saying, *will work for food,* to come and work for me for cash.

My tirade reminds me of the sign in a one man machine shop when I was much younger that read, *lack of planning on your part, does not constitute an emergency on mine.* Over the years that signs meaning has changed for me but I still remember it.

I don't think anyone will ever measure up to impossible standards, not even me. When something goes poorly, I change my requirements, I cut myself some slack. For others I demand perfection and then accept what I get. This line of thinking suggests perhaps I should lower my standards, accept third rate. Hire the hacker. NO!

Fortunately, lots and lots of professionals and contractors have the same issues and strive for excellence in everything they do. So many, in fact that I have been embarrassed by my own unprofessional actions. Kind of puts you in your place when someone truly shines while I am bitching or being difficult to please.

Anyway, as you know, if you want something done right, do it yourself and then lower your standards to match your quality or get someone better than you.

Expert authors and speakers say to under promise and over deliver, I disagree, I think it is better to promise high and then deliver on that promise. Superior associates display this quality when they simply do what they say they will do. How hard is that. The rest just leave you hanging.

As a landlord growing a stable of rentals, you will need to hire and work with people all the time. From the Home Depot special order desk to the real estate professional, all of them affect the bottom line and just as importantly, your frustration level.

When I come across individuals that think and operate at exceptional levels, I tell them so, thank them, reward them, and try to work with them when I can.

Watch the feet

When choosing people to associate with I sometimes think of a lessor rule I have learned to employ. *Watch their feet.* I could have said, seek out others that think the same as you, but to be clear, we all know some people that talk a good show but never do anything. They may think the same way I do, but their feet are firmly planted, not moving, all talk. I deal with these people, I even like most of them, but I recognize they are talkers, not doers. I try not to let them impact me. So I *watch their feet*, to see if they walk the talk.

> *Throughout the book are rules, I think of them as suggestions, or reminders, not direct orders from above.*

Partnerships

I said at this books beginning that I have strong opinions, that is not to say I don't believe there are other ways than my way or the highway. I think everyone should do what works for them. It is their vision and big picture not mine.

I mention Linda a lot, I say us, our and we interchangeably because we are partners. I think spouses and landlording are partnerships made for each other. Friends being partners in owning a hand full of houses, I just can't see it unless they hire management for everything, then they aren't really landlords. In our kind of rental business, we are hands on including maintenance, Linda and I share the work according to our abilities. I run the concrete pavement breakers because I am bigger/stronger, but she ran her half of a two person earth auger once when we built a playground. (I slipped and let go leaving her being dragged in a circle. It was kinda funny but not for her. In my opinion partners are a team with a common goal.

We have been in limited partnerships, but that's totally different. In our case we borrowed private money for a project and paid our limited partner interest after completion. Having an expanding mortgage where you don't make payments until you sell out would be a good description.

My only true partner is Linda, she is right there with me in the thick of things and neither of us (I hope) feels treated unfairly. We are in it together, win, lose or tie, and share the pain. Contrast what I just said with any partnership you know about, I bet you have heard some complaining. When we complain it is about the work not each other. (mostly)

> Taking advice *matters,* the key is, *take advice*

Family involvement

Our kids grew up as the children of landlords. Not by choice but by birth, they hung around rentals from purchase to remodel to tenant, to do it again. They learned to paint and they learned that things can be fixed. They also learned a little politics.

I stressed to the kids not to talk at school or sports activities about our family business. I did this because from time to time we got negative feedback from parents. More than once when conversation with another parent touched on renting I would hear disparaging anti landlord remarks. Things like "money grubbing assxxxx," tend to make you hide your true identity. For me it was easy, I said I know what you mean, I'm a handyman and work for those jerks. All true. Or I admit to being in property management and repairs and leave it at that.

I also tried to make our children understand that if they told friends that we owned mountain and beach houses and homes down the street that they would come across as snotty rich kids. Far far from it.

The plain truth is and was, is that we made considerably less money than most of the other parents. What we had though was our foot in the door of a great business investment that would one day allow us to reap rewards. Another hard to quantify but very real benefit was what most self employed enjoy. The ability to schedule work around family if they desire and we desired that very much. Once when I was patting myself on my own back, I told Linda that as well as I could remember, neither of us had ever missed being at home with our kids at bedtime or in the morning or missing any school or scouting event our children wanted us to attend with them.

Teaching our children skills

I am not advocating landlording as a skill or life's profession to be taught to our children, I'm not against it either. Our family doesn't qualify as a scientific study but we included our kids in everything appropriate at our rentals. They painted at three, when their help was truly a hindrance and made jobs take twice as long. They spackled and spread drywall compound at six and then I fixed it. They roofed, cleaned and pruned too. At a a beach rental, all nine of us knocked out a total re-roof job in a short weekend once. Of course they were older then.

Today as adults the seven of them display talents for multiple construction crafts and virtually any home maintenance issues. They all have can-do attitudes that are essential for any project life throws at them. Being landlord's kids hasn't hurt them in the least, most have solid careers and degrees.

I meet old and young today that are unable to do anything for themselves. In fact our society seems to churn out followers that have embraced an attitude that one must be an expert or hire an expert for everything. Worse yet, it has become a badge of distinction to be viewed as helpless. I think these people are dead weight and will be voted off the island first, second and third.

I remember insisting my oldest son make a paper pattern and then using shears cut the new vinyl for a bathroom floor. How he complained and carried on was sad, almost bringing me to tears along with him. He was so worried he would make a mistake. Then he spread the adhesive with a notched trowel and flopped and rolled the material. It turned out perfect, a job well done for both of us. He remembers that day and says I was mean to him. Today, he prefers tile and I learn tricks from him. I have similar children stories involving concrete, electrical, finish work, framing, plumbing, the list is endless. None of my children will be first voted off, heck they may be the only ones that know how to vote.

Like I said I don't advocate landlording as a basic skill to learn or teach our children but a one trick pony is limited in today's world. In our family the wings have spread and talents are dispersed to all fields, from teaching to high tech to construction. The incomes they are earning are allowing all of them to become homeowners and landlords.

In a way I envy my kids and all people with disposable income getting into rental ownership today. I wish it were me back then instead of raking leaves, but we all make choices and then play the hands dealt.

What do kids remember

Recently I asked my daughter that is now on her second rental what she remembers about growing up a landlord kid. I was trolling for stories to put in this book. She immediately said the smell. I was expecting to hear about cool toys she found when helping clean out empty houses. My son who was visiting and has one rental piped up, yeah the smell, and added, all the times mom was worried when you worked in a bad area after dark to fix something or collect rent.

I wasn't getting anywhere on my book material. My daughter, still on smell offered, it smelled like that yellow sofa you brought home. "What are you talking about, brought home," I said. Linda jumped in with, "that yellow one with the wood legs you bought at the thrift store." "For our House?" I said completely confused. "Yes, you brought it home for us and we made you get rid of it."

Apparently at the time we were not rolling in cash and I found something I liked at a thrift store, but the family rejected it. Conveniently I don't have any memory of the incident.

Picking a mentor

Oops, the title suggests picking a mentor may be simple and that there is an all knowing guru out there just for you. That's lazy thinking. In my life, a mentor is anyone that has practical first hand experience that I may learn from. But I draw some distinctions. For example a down in the dumps homeless person that once was on top of the world has all sorts of experience, but he obviously made some bad choices so I listen with a grain of salt and maybe learn what he did wrong so I don't repeat his mistakes. I learn from successful individuals. This means a twenty something blog writer or graduate of management 101 cannot possibly have the experience or wisdom of a fifty, sixty or seventy year old self-made business magnate. I doubt very much the thirty something professor teaching a course can hold a candle to a seasoned CEO either.

I can feel the breeze from feathers I just ruffled so let me explain. In my opinion anyone can teach or learn how to screen a tenant, or rate a credit score or fill in a rental condition check list. It takes no talent to document things and pick a tenant from a list of applicants. I am not diminishing classes or school, but It is no secret how any of the busy work is completed. That is what is taught, just read any online search result for rental management classes. They are mostly the same basic common sense curriculum. Who knew? The mentors I have benefited from most, talk from real world personal experience.

My best mentor advice has come from those that I respect for their achievements and success. I have met individuals that have buckets of money and too many homes to manage by themselves. Those are the ones I want to have coffee with.

> *Mentors are where you find them*

No mentor knows it all. In landlording, I needed construction and repair wisdom from a builder type person, I needed financial advice, not from a CPA, from a person experienced in risking their own money, someone who had been there and done that.

My CPA mentor came along when we started doing exchanges and depreciation. I never considered asking her about first and last months rent or damage deposits.

Believe it or not I have learned a lot from radio shows but I don't drink it all in. That's lazy thinking again. I do my own thinking.

Mentors are everywhere, I think we can learn from them all. Mentors may be the homeless living a lifestyle resulting from poor choices to the successful tycoon setting a high bar to strive for..

I think it is fun to talk clichés and myth's. Many are born of some sort of truth or reality and unfortunately have become engrained in peoples lives. Lets dispel some that affect real estate thinking.

I takes money to make money, sound familiar? On the same order is, *pay to play.* It's true that money helps but there are substitutes for money. Sweat equity comes to mind and what about no money down private contracts?

Once in a lifetime opportunity. This cliché can easily be true, the problem is it plays on emotion, it suggests immediacy and may cause a rash decision throwing common sense out the window. Savvy salesman use this tool successfully.

All the good deals are gone - this is not cliché or myth it's just baloney, this is a quitters excuse for not even looking.

Real estate agents, attorneys, escrow, cc and r's, rules and regulations are for your protection. There is a place for all of them, but you are ultimately responsible. These people all have cya papers for you to sign. CYA means cover your ass, it is mostly their rear not your rear that is being covered.

Myths are invented ideas, story's, concepts. Cliches are over used sayings. The problem with dumb myths and over used cliches is that they can cause people to not think things through. Cliches invoke shortcut thinking and then people make poor decisions that affect all of us.

Here is an example we hear on the news everyday. The commentator during his spiel will say *"clearly"* as in *"clearly the sky is falling,"* saying *clearly* dismisses any question that it may not be falling because clearly it is. Another one is *"without a doubt,"* when someone says, *"the house is without a doubt solid as a rock,"* you don't think or wonder if it is true, after all he said *without a doubt*, so it must be solid as a rock.

What happens in real estate is, people tend to use myths and cliches to convince others to come to a certain conclusion. We take it in without ever questioning the veracity. *Clearly,* that's *without a doubt* lazy thinking. The cynic in me spots these red flag myths and cliches as manipulative tools. Sometimes it will suddenly dawn on me that the person speaking to me is really very good at it, but is quite full of it too. Then, I reassess everything they have said. I would expect you to be doing the same with this book.

More to ponder:
- A fool and his money are soon parted
- The value is in the land
- Market timing is crucial
- We are all on the same team
- Rising tides lift all boats
- Buy quality
- Most people are trustworthy
- Real estate is risky
- Risk reward ratio

Some old favorites.. *Winners never quit and quitters never win. When you assume. Sell the sizzle. To be honest or with all due respect. The fact of the matter is. Win win. Brings value to the table. At the end of the day. Putting lipstick on a pig.* And lastly, *net net,* what ever that means.

I had fun putting the last essay together, I hope you enjoyed it. I found myself having cynical thoughts while writing it. I'm not sure where I stand or rank myself on the cynicism scale or if it even matters.

Good times and good life

You may think after reading pages from this book that landlording is nothing but conflict and evictions and repairing tenant inflicted damages. It is not. Owning rentals is a business and like many business owners we chart our own path and future. With that statement said, I know some landlords don't run their rentals strictly business like, they buy a house find a tenant and that's the last they think of it. Perhaps that is the beauty of owning rentals, you really can be absent and still make a buck.

While writing this one sided tell all book, I became concerned that I was depicting the landlord business in the worst possible way. What should I write about? Rent arriving on time every month? Tenants acting normal? Faucets that don't drip? Readers would get bored and put this book away if I wrote about the months, stretching to years of nothing happening. Or I could write how we went on winter cruises to Mexico, all nine of us. And no tenants knew we were out of the country. How we were able to go to soccer games, scout outings and drag all our children off to Hawaii. No that would be boring as I sense it has become right now.

At some point in this book, and I guess this is the point, I wanted to dispel the myth that *it takes money to make money,* we started out broke without jobs. We stayed broke for a long time. We struggled to pay our bills and cover mortgages. When the kids were little, we recycled newsprint and hauled scrap metal to get by but we stuck it out and made it work for us. As we acquired more homes, we began to benefit from the economic flywheel I describe as the float. Eventually, we began to enjoy some spendable cash flow but I worked part time, first as a handyman, then as an excavator supporting our family. Our rentals were a long time evolving into a smooth running clock work that support us today. Was it worth it? For us, heck yes. For you? That's for you to decide.

Chapter 2

Golden Rule
for Acquiring Property

Simple universal rule.

"Never stop being a buyer." Sounds too simplistic doesn't it? Hear me out, suppose you go home and refuse to answer the phone after 7pm as some people do, (I knew an attorney once that told me he had an aversion to talking business on weekends, that means that he was not in his market for two days a week.) you may miss a great deal. That is fine, many agree with that thinking, including me, but I am not looking for property right now. I'm not in the market. As such, I don't expect to come across any deals either. To acquire property or anything else one must be open and looking 100% of the time. Deals don't come along just during bankers hours five days a week while taking Friday afternoons off. When Monday rolls around last week is gone and so is the deal you never knew about.

> *Never stop looking is the secret*
> *to acquiring property*

If that simple example didn't light your fire, I will bet three tacos and a coke that you thought of some lame excuse for why you can't buy anything today, last weekend or this very moment. Bad credit, no credit, low pay, no pay, no down payment. The list is endless and phoney. *The real reason you can't acquire something right now is because you aren't a buyer, you quit looking or never began..*

Now, I'm not in a million years suggesting you can and will get your dream. What I am saying is you can't ever, ever, get anything by making excuses for inaction. You must be in the market and looking, not every minute of every day but you can't stop being a buyer. When you stop, it's over. You must be in the market even if you have no idea where you are headed or how to get there. I cannot emphasize this enough. If you are financially challenged it is absolutely essential that you get out there or you will miss that perfect no money down deal.

> Open
> For
> business

> Closed

Pick one

My second golden rule deal came after selling my first home.

As luck would have it, a work acquaintance told me about a for sale property with acreage out in the country on the side of Mt Hood. Forested with a clear mountain stream flowing through the middle. I needed a place to live so off I went in a hurry, a big hurry, It was thirty five miles from work but I was laid off a lot back then so driving was not a big deal. The house was an unfinished cabin, no plumbing, no interior, no heat and that's the good part. The bad part was that the owner builder had built it five feet over the property line on the neighbors property, and then had a well drilled on the neighbors land as well. It gets better, the builder was in prison and wasn't getting out for a long time. A relative was handling the property.

It never occurred to me to look into getting conventional financing, the home was not habitable, the well was capped, the driller had not been paid, lawsuits were in the air, and the neighbor was rightfully pissed.

I made simultaneous private contract offers to both owners, each contingent on the acceptance of the other. In a few days when the dust had settled, I was digging an outhouse under a cedar tree next to my new home on six and half acres.

Never stop being a buyer.

Let's look at the deal. You may think I lucked out, that's debatable. What is not in question was that I was actively looking for a place to buy. I dropped everything to go check it out. The two owners needed a solution to the property line encroachment. I made an immediate offer within my meager means that addressed their needs. The offer was accepted.

Now as I think back to 1976, that purchase was the first time I employed my universal rule about buying real estate. For years and years since then, I have preached to my children and anyone that will listen what the one simple rule they could follow that will guarantee they acquire property. *Never stop being a buyer.* So simple yet so true.

You can close this book right now, I just told you my secret to buying property. Of course if you keep reading you may pick up a few pointers and ideas on how to rent out and hang on to your hard earned good fortune.

Picking the perfect property when broke.

We knew in the beginning that we had few actual choices in a world of many choices. It is easy to romanticize what you want to buy but reality soon sets in and you realize that you only have one or two viable options. For example, a deal for no money down and a fair interest rate comes along. I have two choices, #1, take the deal including all the baggage that comes with it, or #2, pass. What would you do?

We did both many times. Of course we turned down dumb deals, and just as important we sold, traded or gave away deals that weren't working for us. Always the pragmatist and with lots of property available because I never quit being a buyer, I learned to size up potential properties fast. I employ the same method today. I begin by assuming I will be buying the property or somehow moving forward. Next, I look for deal breakers. Deal breakers are exactly that, any issue that is insurmountable. I don't give the house a second thought once a deal breaker has surfaced. Why waste my time. If the owner or agent says a three year balloon payment is not negotiable, I say thank you and walk out the door. If during a walk through I discover a structural issue I am not willing to tackle, I don't continue, that's it.

I have had my family question my system saying things like, don't you want to know what's in the bedroom closet. I say no, I don't want to waste my time, I'm only looking for deal breakers, everything else I will deal with later or repair. To be honest, after I find zero deal breakers, I pay more attention to little things but not to decide if I'm interested in the property, remember I already said I assume I am buying it. I look at it more closely because I will soon be making remodel and repair decisions. At that point I will be making measurements and taking lots of pictures. It is amazing how hard it is to accurately remember details, pictures are really important when I buy and rent.

I sense I should clarify. In spite of what the gurus say, when you are broke you buy what is available to you, you don't have many

34

choices or bargaining power. You must say no as I said to deal breakers but saying yes is how we did it.

I haven't talked money, you should know or estimate all your numbers. Don't leave out little things like pruning that pretty fruit tree or mowing the lawn between tenants. Those little numbers will bite you. When we started out, we thought if we forecast $100 cash flow per month we would come out okay. We were wrong, now with thirty five years experience we know that planning for $200 positive cash flow was a closer number. That means we barely broke even, the $100 or $200 was all used up in unplanned or under budgeted expenses. Once again, we were off by $200 per month every time. I expect readers of this book will benefit from our lessons and do better than we did but I will bet that they still under estimate. We learned to expect the unexpected.

We mostly do all our own maintenance, this definitely keeps the costs down and the profits in our pocket. Hiring help may push your rental into negative cash flow. If your day job can afford the hits you can ride out the ups and downs, but eventually your rent income must pay the bills. For us, it took about ten years before we surfaced.

If your plan is to flip empty houses, you will need considerably more capitol since you will have no income. We have never bought a home solely to flip it. We have flipped a number of homes after renting for a few years but they were exchanges for better rentals.

> *Landlording is like driving a car or boat.*
> *They all take you to a destination but steering*
> *takes you to your chosen destination..*

Managing rentals is as much a personal statement as a financial strategy. The end result is your public image to own up to or make excuses for. The reality is most of us don't get to pick and choose, we can't buy or manage everything we want. Our cash, **35** credit, perseverance, resources, the big picture, all determine our rentals and what our portfolio looks like, not what we wanted it to look like. I think for most of us, the more broke we are, the fewer our choices so there is no perfect property, just left overs. Our left overs provided a foundation to build upon and today support us.

We bought run down shacks at first because they were easy to acquire with little or no cash. A high income earner may buy a mini mansion as his first rental. We might have bought ten houses for what that guy invested in one house. Both are excellent strategy's that fit a particular situation. We made our hundred year old shanty's nice and took care to meet our tenants security and comfort needs. The other guy must do the same.

The palace may double in value due to the areas overall appreciation but rent may be hard to increase in an area of owner occupied mansions. The rundown hovel may increase ten fold due to remodeling followed by rent increases and area appreciation. When comparing returns and cash spent, being broke is hard to beat but what choice do you have. Did I just say being broke is hard to beat when comparing returns? - Yes.

I hear others and wannabe's in the rental business lobby for mansions, multiples, single family, fixers, flipping, the list is as long as the MLS pages. They say landlords must actively do this and that, blah blah blah. I do the same talking myselft is entertaining and even self justifies the decisions we have made. I think it is natural to paint your own choices and outcomes favorably, who wants to admit they are broke, make mistakes or intentionally own old shacks.

Picking the perfect property when not broke.

If you stick it out long enough, your houses will get paid off or you will trade or refinance creating some cash needing a new home. Or maybe you start out with some cash. Wow lucky you. In any case having a few bucks greatly increases the field of choices open to you. You can actually make some smart decisions and go out and find exactly what you want. That is if you know what you want.

If you go online or read books you will find huge numbers of authors telling you step by step what to do and how to choose a house. Upon scrutiny you will find they all say pretty much the same thing. Things like, consider the homes condition, be sure to check the crime rate and hire an expert inspection. I won't go on but the list is both exhausting and pretty useless because none of them tell you what to do. In my opinion, many articles are not written by landlords, managers or even property owners. They are just writers filling space, or blogger's mining the Internet for clicks.

My choices for rentals are suited for me but I'm experienced and buy what I am comfortable with. I probably have a lower vacancy rate than most landlords and spend less on repairs because I know construction and hire myself if possible.

This is what I do. I think we are all niche thinkers and lookers, meaning we have specifics wants in a rental. I want four bedrooms because they bring significantly more rent than three. I will consider two or three bedroom places if I see a way forward in a remodel. This means I need to schedule a time slot in our family life that will allow me remodeling time as well as a suitable subject property. Simply putting a bed in a basement is not acceptable. Bedrooms must have legal ingress and egress, they must have a closet and not be much less than one hundred square feet I want to be able to honestly advertise four bedrooms.

I want a minimum of one and a half bathrooms, and again I look for remodel potential. Remodeling is important for us, it adds instant value and boosts the rent. I try to stay away from expensive furnace and roof replacements and concrete redo's but I don't mind popping in new vinyl windows.

I am not a fan of tile or marble counters unless I plan to sell soon.

I know some landlords are sold on glitzy glamour saying it draws more rent and better tenants., I disagree, I think it is mostly wasted money and setting one up for expensive repairs. I want bullet proof properties that will stand the test of many decades.

When I consider a house for a rental I visit the street and neighborhood first. I park near by or in front. I might walk around several blocks. I am eager to talk with anyone I meet. If I am uncomfortable or fear anything at all in my reconnoiter of the neighborhood I will strongly reconsider. I also think about my wife and children and how they would feel. My kids are grown now but they all grew up playing in our rental neighborhoods. The places we had that were uncomfortable, we got rid of and as I look back now, I know that was the correct decision for us.

You can and should do some checking of crime and other statistics online but I think on foot in person is important. Next, I walk the yard. I'm looking for water flow problems when it rains forty days and nights. I'm looking for flooding potential, I'm looking for nosey neighbors because I want to talk with them. I'm looking at roofs and gutters, siding and windows. I'm looking for concrete issues. I want to see lots of clearance below siding and above the ground. I'm looking for major yard work that I don't want to deal with, (a 100 foot tree will cost $5,000 to bring down) I'm looking at expensive fencing, I'm looking for potential deal breakers. Lastly I'm looking for upgrade potential that will substantially increase value and rent and rentability. I try to do my walk around by myself, without Linda or an agent or owner, otherwise I get distracted.

I make my way back to the front entrance, it is important to enter the way your tenants will enter. I open and close the door from both inside and outside, I inspect the weather stripping. I consider stormy weather and look for trip hazards at the entry. Again, I try to be alone, I'm the one that's going to be fixing things. I take a deep breath and smell, I try to imagine my renter, what are they thinking right now if they were standing in the entry. Next I walk through the entire house, I'm looking for obvious defects of course but also I'm looking

38 for things a renter will complain about. I can fix an ugly wall or floor but I can't make a bedroom bigger. Lots of tenants double or triple up kids with more beds or bunks. A three bedroom house with small bedrooms and no way to easily remedy is very close to a deal breaker for me. While I'm looking at a houses I am thinking of section eight requirements, for instance, single pane windows reduce section eight rent substantially, stairways and railings must be the approved style. I open and close and latch all the windows and doors, after all, I may be back the day after closing to fix them, I need to know how much work to expect. I'm also looking for telltale settling evident in doorways. Settling scares away novices, but is probably not a deal breaker for me. Settling issues are a really good way to knock down the price. I look for sloppy remodeling and code violations I will have to address, another good way to knock down the price.

If it looks like I am interested in the home I will pull out my tape and measure bedrooms, bathrooms, and things I may want to discuss with Linda, I try to take pictures of things that may be issues or that we should discuss later.

I don't tell the agent or owner I am excited or even interested if I plan to make an offer. The easiest money I have ever made was when I have bought houses at a discounted price, not when I sold them. The buying and price offering calculations begin when I drive down the street. Even though I try to look without distractions, I make a point of asking the agent or owner questions about things I notice. Chances are, I know all I need to know and I am probably better versed in repairs than they are but I ask simple questions in hopes of learning secrets and softening resistance to a low offer I may make.

If I am only luke warm about the property, I may talk it, over with Linda, but looking at other property probably is where we are headed. Though it is considered not good to get emotionally involved over rentals, I think one should like and want a property. If you don't care at all about a place perhaps it is an indicator you should keep looking.

I don't forget that sooner or later I will be selling what I buy, or my heirs will. I never fail to ask myself, will this property sell well as is or with remodeling. That is not to say a rental must be a hot seller for me to be interested. We have owned houses that were very difficult to sell but easy to rent for a good return. I simply think it is a prudent consideration to think about selling before I buy.

That is how I size up a prospective new rental property. Notice I have said nothing about rents. The reason is because I already know what rent I can expect based upon the number of bedrooms, square footage, location and general condition. I have done my homework, I am not wasting my time looking at houses that won't work for me.

I will sum up this process with a less than profound analogy. *Landlording is like driving a car or boat. They all take you to a destination but steering takes you to your chosen destination..*

I assume I will be buying a property,
I look for deal breakers
saving the closet inspections for later.

Landlords don't flip homes or do they

We observed in our thirty years raising children and talking among other parents that just about everyone either has a rental or used to have one, or wanted one. The rest had poor opinions about landlords in general. Most were happy to tell us how horrible being a landlord is, or some disaster that cost them their sanity and their savings. Many equated being a landlord with flipping homes, a comparison that I find insulting. The flippers often made a one time killing and bragged about it. In my opinion those people confuse landlording with speculation and gambling.

I have said we never bought a home planning to flip it, however you would be irresponsible not to think about selling before you make your first offer. That's correct, ask yourself if you can sell it tomorrow if you make a mistake, or will you be stuck for ten years or more before surfacing for air.

This book is not about flipping but we need the talk anyway. The common misconception is that you make all your money when you sell the property. That is only partially correct, in my way of thinking, I make money when I buy the house. I don't overpay, I look for upside potential appreciation. I look for remodel or fixer potential. I do not want the nicest house in the neighborhood. Above all else I want the house that (after it is upgraded) is wanted by everyone else, renters and buyers alike. If I make the correct choice in the beginning, I will get maximum rent and sooner or later I will receive the money I made back on day one when I bought the house.

Planning for the long term

When we started in the eighties as wannabe rental titans, we bought our first house because we could, we didn't buy a strip mall because we couldn't. When we had the chance to acquire multiples we jumped on it because we could. Then, a light went on in the attic and we found ourselves managing both single family and multiples. Right away Linda began sensing she didn't like having tenants calling us at all hours to complain about other tenants. We **41** didn't enjoy the dumpster squabbles and parking wars. Then, we found out tenant A's porch light was on tenant B's meter. It was easy for us to quit considering multiples. Notice, I have said nothing about the superior cash flow and return on investment that multiples are famous for. I choose my future for more than ROI. Multiples are not in it, at least for now. Watch out for the expert advice touting cash flow and ROI that ignore management. Income and ROI are what you get out of your investment but management is the work one must do everyday to earn that money.

Look at it this way - You are buying a job, a job you can't easily quit or call in sick. You are not buying ROI. Confusing the two is a shocker for those that don't think it out.

Bedrooms for rent

We discovered early on that the more bedrooms a property has, the more rent it demands. This seems like such an obvious truth it makes me wonder why a landlord would even consider buying a one or two bedroom house. If you read expert advice books this little point is glossed over or not brought up in favor of location, location, location, curb appeal, condition and price. You should not make the mistake of thinking a great location will make up for lack of bedrooms.

If all things are equal, a 1050 sq ft two bedroom home will sell for the same as a 1050 sq ft three bedroom maybe even a little more because bigger rooms show better. The three bedroom home will rent for more every time, and when it comes time to sell, the three bedroom will have more potential buyers.

I recommend doing what we have done, and that is survey two, three, and four bedroom for rent ads. Separate them by economic areas and chart the results. We found that several hundred rent dollars separated each choice. We also noticed very little difference with having garages, yards, family rooms or extra bathrooms. Bedrooms rule the rent world.

Most of our homes we bought because of opportunity, not because we had the pick of the litter. But we sold or traded away two bedroom homes that did not provide a good rent return, or required horrendous attention on our part. The end result is that we ended up with a stable of long term rentals we still have today.

We employed remodeling many times to add bedrooms. Our first rental was Sam's house, a two bedroom with unfinished basement and full headroom (in the middle) attic with a nice access stairway. You guessed it, in between tenants I framed in a family room and bedroom downstairs. I increased the rent by $200 and had my pick of applicants. Later I wired and dry walled the attic during another vacancy upping the rent again.

Much much later, we sold the four bedroom house, and had our pick of buyers .

Lucky breaks

Lets put this to bed once and for all, there are lucky breaks but luck has nothing to do with it. I will quote the person in our history credited with summing it all up. A Roman Philosopher named Seneca said, "Luck Is What Happens When Preparation Meets Opportunity." This means many things, my take is that we make our own luck by being prepared. By extension, I think that the more prepared you are, the better your potential for very good luck. Now lets reverse the scenario. You don't work weekends or answer the phone after seven, you also don't make offers because you think you have nothing, no gold to offer. If I described you, you owe me some tacos and can expect bad luck. (If confused, see pg 33 for Taco ref.)

The next page has one last borrowed worn out rule I preached to my kids when they were little.

Perseverance rules

Winners never quit and quitters never win. Technically a true statement, but for this book, I am pounding home the mindset that you must get out there and stay out there. If you do, you will stumble on something, get lucky, call it what ever you want. If you don't do it, I give up - you can have the tacos, its your lucky day after all.

Now that we have hammered home the 'Never quit rule lets go in to it further for those that still see fault. As your resources include less gold, so will your deals, that should be obvious. Don't expect the Tag Mahal or a strip mall on a contract with no down payment. You can expect a fixer that the bank has sneered at or someone's problem waiting for your solution. If you accurately assess your gold, and never quit looking, your time will be well spent. If you lie to yourself or expect something for nothing, you will dig a hole to wallow in. Remember, gold is not always counted in dollars. I have proved that to myself many times.

> *A person's gold is all their assets,*
> *whether cash - credit - intellectual -*
> *or just plain hard work.*

Chapter 3
It's All About Money

Get rich quick in rentals

Getting rich quick is the stuff of dreams and radio show hucksters but getting rich is a distinct possibility for landlords. I will say it again, this is not a flipping book but flipping is part of being an active landlord. We focused on collecting rents but in the process we learned as anyone would that our property's needed to be shuffled because we weren't that smart and picked some losers. Some purchases we made were because we took advantage of deals, not because we necessarily liked the choice. Some purchases were out and out mistakes. Most property we sold/flipped was to reallocate our assets for family and business goals.

So the above paragraph explains why flipping was part of ours or anyone's big picture. In more detail; you flip a property to buy more property, you flip a property because it sucks as a rental or needs more work than you want to do. If you sell a property because you want to have the cash, then you are not a landlord anymore and have quit being a real estate investor. If you quit being an investor you also have no chance, none, of getting richer than you are. To be an investor you must own or control property, it is as simple as that.

> *If you sell your property you have quit being an investor and have no chance of becoming richer than you already are.*

I have never pushed my kids into landlording but I have strongly suggested they should own their own homes. All of us have read the articles gurus write about renting versus owning. They **45** invariably show charts and graphs and quote economists citing statistics where for a full decade people would be better off as a renter instead of owning or vice versa. What they fail to point out is that as a renter there is no possible upside, as a home owner the upside is tremendous. The downside is that you may have some repairs and may be marginally better off as a renter for a period, not forever.

Impossible to quantify is the pride of ownership and stability not having a landlord brings to home ownership.

Lastly, if all else fails to move your dial, *regular savings* has been drummed into us since we were little. "Pay yourself first," payroll deduction, are all savings tricks to build that nest egg. A mortgage is paying yourself first in spades. After thirty years of forced savings even the worst money managers will have a tidy asset built up.

Losing focus is losing money

We all know Ben Franklin's quote, "A penny saved is a penny earned." Researching that quote surprised me, it turns out back in the early days they spoke differently and Ben never said it exactly that way. According to scholars that have read Poor Richards Almanac, he wrote, "A penny saved is two pence clear," and also, "A penny saved is a penny got."

For my purposes the modern version is sufficient. Throughout this book I have related stories and made comments about construction and rental management where money is wasted. Ben Franklin goes on to explain that saving a penny is twice as beneficial, he said that the penny lost was earned first, and then must be replaced by earning it again, hence 2x I guess.

Running my rental business is just like any business in that I must pay the bills. One day I was giving unsolicited advice to an owner of a resale clothing shop that was losing money everyday but still had lots more to lose. My advice was, pretend to accelerate time and act as if the cash capital is already exhausted, meaning pretend you are dead broke today. Now make decisions as if truly dead broke. I have been in similar situations, we all have to some degree.

Remember the time at the store when you forgot your credit card and your wallet. All you had was a little mad money or change. (Yes No) I do, I was forced to trim purchases and get only the most important item I could afford, the rest of my purchases had to wait until I came back with more dough. Running a broke business is the same, you must trim costs and expenses or the business will soon be gone. What is wrong with not wasting money or cutting costs? It is undoubtedly the easiest most cost effective way to make money. Ben said it best, it pays 2X or two pence clear.

I don't kid myself, it is all about money. Some new managers and some wealthy managers don't understand this basic rule. Over paying or paying for something unnecessarily is just plain dumb or being disingenuous with yourself. If I am wrong on this point, then I need to rethink why I own rental property, I've always thought it was to make a living and one day retire. It's all about money!

> *"A Penney Saved is a Penney earned."*
>
> *Ben F*

I'm not quite done with my penny saving rant. I mentioned wealthy managers for a reason. I have seen it in others, in myself and my family. When things are going good, bills are paid, cash is thrown off to buy toys and then we get hit with an extra expense, we tend to minimize in our head, the cost. I guess it is because we can afford it. It's not busting the bank. I saw it recently with my son, he mentioned an unexpected rental expense saying it was only a grand. I never said anything to him but I thought, *only a grand - a thousand bucks - my gosh that's two weeks pay, that was your Montessori school payment for three months.* I really did think all those things. My take is that people with money and inexperienced new managers don't fully appreciate **47** they are running a business with profit and loss. No profit no business.

The new inexperienced manager must learn to watch the nickels or go broke getting educated. The wealthy manager/owner can afford to lose on his rentals because he makes his money doing something else. He may be a landlord and real estate investor but this book is more about making property pay its own way and providing income.

When the wealthy guy does his taxes he benefits from depreciation deductions or when he sells he makes a killing on appreciation. Either way he is making money in real estate so it is hard to find fault with what works.

I guess I am little jealous.

Monthly payment trap

This is old news, but getting buried in monthly bills is a subject lots of us know about. It is all too easy to do with pre approved credit cards coming in the mail three of four at a time. Every one with a low teaser interest rate for six months. Also an unbelievably high credit limit (fine print - if you qualify). Some bank offers I have received give you the deal only if you transfer a balance from a competitor bank which is kind of a underhanded dirty trick if you think about it.

So we have established that easy expensive credit is out there for the taking. The problem is that if you are already using all your credit based on your ability to make monthly payments, you should not be digging deeper. Having a rental needing repairs or needing to make a mortgage payment while it is vacant is a strong motivation to keep on charging. I know I have been there and I have done exactly that. It is a risky business that incrementally sneaks up on landlords.

Getting in over ones head leads to an emergency bailing out sale which brings on another mistake. That mistake is pinning all your hopes on one event. Even if an emergency sale is put together it takes two months to close while the bills pile up. All this misery may be avoided by not over extending. It's easy to say but tough to do but you must do it to succeed.

I have said before I never make a deal I can't live with forever. I learned that the hard way before I adopted the motto. This is why it is so important to get that daily rent. When my rentals go vacant, I know I can't pay the mortgage out of my pocket for long so I make my top priority getting a new tenant in place. Lets be honest, the new tenant will have first and last months rent and a deposit and that really helps the cash shortage, but more importantly, next month you get rent income again instead of feeding the money pit another month.

We learned to not bet on the future by over extending our credit. Today, we still pay cash whenever possible. It is a tough call and may slow growth, even cause you to defer maintenance but it is cheap insurance that keeps you in the game when others are failing.

We were about ten years into landlording before our cash flow took a positive turn due to rent hikes. Up to then I was working long hours supporting our homes but I could see the results in our balance sheet. I knew we were building equity across the board.

The Economic Flywheel

Being a landlord means handling money. More property, more money. Much if not all the money is not yours because it is earmarked to pay the bills or is in trust for your tenants. Never the less, the money is in your account. I call it reserves. I set aside money to pay property taxes and insurance and I collect deposits and last months rent. Some quick math shows surprising results. Ten security or cleaning deposits of $1,000 each is ten grand, ten last months rent at an average of $1,500 each is fifteen more. Ten property taxes saved up for half a year might be another twenty grand. My example adds up to $45,000. I coined the term economic flywheel to describe this pile of cash that is in constant flux in my accounts.

I do not think there is much chance I will need to pay all the deposits and apply all the last months rents at the same time. If I need a thousand for an emergency repair, I borrow it from myself. I don't kid myself, it is not my money. I have a responsibility to remain solvent. Judging from stories I have heard from disgruntled ex landlords, not everyone remains solvent, they don't maintain reserves, they borrow and spend their equity. They get in trouble of their own making.

When we began we struggled to keep things rolling along. Negative or zero cash flow left us little cushion, but as we grew, rents caught up, vacancies went down and we handled more money, our economic flywheel grew as well.

In business, money in flux is called float. Economic flywheel is my term for money in trust or ear marked for taxes. We give ourselves short term interest free loans. Local laws may not allow commingling tenant money with personal money especially for landlords with larger complexes or many properties. In any case I would be very cautious borrowing against money earmarked and set aside.

I would like to add, we have never looked at our real estate investment property as separate from our personal home or our family obligations. Our lives have always been one big basket, paying a rental bill is just as important as paying any personal bill. It should be clear that collecting the daily rent is also personal, and just as important as my work income.

Return on investment cash cows

ROI is not hard to calculate but seems to be confusing when I read about it. Maybe I don't do it right, or maybe I think differently. I think of the cash or my effort put into a deal or rental is my investment, that's the I. The return or R is what I get back. If I put in $1,000 and get back $1,000 in a year I have a 100% return or 100% divided by 12 = 8.3% per month average. This is very simple and easy to understand and is called cash on cash ROI. If I put up a $50,000 down payment and get back the same measley grand which is not enough to cover my expenses, I am unhappy and experiencing huge negative cash flow. If I sell out for a lot more than I paid, I will then have a totally improved ROI. What if I can't sell and run out of money? In that case I made a really dumb mistake and lost my family's money.

I ran that last scenario by you to emphasize that putting up a big chunk of cash may get you a deal but not a guaranteed outcome. I wont do a deal unless I have the wherewithal to absorb all negatives and can stick it out to the grave. In other words, I won't bet or gamble, trying strike it rich.

Back to ROI. Making a high target return has never meant much to me. Never losing money, building equity and income is my goal. I have had some losing rentals that if I bailed would have resulted in a loss, or more likely a loss of all my hard work. By sticking it out this has never happened and never will. Much more agreeable are the rentals that fall into my lap and spew out dollars year after year. Real cash cows.

I have told this next great success story many times for many reasons, sometimes accentuating certain parts to make a point but mostly to brag.

One of my landlord customers called and said, "Remember that house on Raymond street that you worked on about nine months ago," I said, "sorry, but not really." "Sure you do," he said, "over by the pizza place on 82nd, you put new vinyl in the kitchen."

Now, I remembered it. It was a big kitchen with a monster seam down the middle. He was offering to sell me the house. The price was fair but the terms were irresistible. Nothing down, payments at 10.5% apr amortized over 30 years. The first payment due thirty days after closing and he would cover the escrow fees. The house was vacant, he would mail me the key today so Linda and I could take a look.

To this day, that's the best return on investment I have done, but it gets better. When I took Linda to look at the house, I knew we would be buying it so I brought a for rent sign and planted it on the corner by the pizza place. The old house checked out okay. We could have spiffed it up but not this time. When we got home that evening I had a message from a prospective tenant. The next morning I met the person at the house and rented it to her. She paid me first and last months rent and the deposit. I took my for rent sign home and added the new key to my key box.

If you have been tracking the story, I have had possession, or at least the key, for less than twenty four hours, I have two months rent and the deposit in my pocket. By the time we went to closing, I collected a third months rent and still haven't made my first payment. The tenant ended up staying for over five years. My only maintenance was replacing the water heater in year four.

So here is the math problem, I have no cash in this deal, I have a healthy positive cash flow and no vacancy for five years - what is my return on investment?

A penny saved

I have talked about getting the daily rent. Some might think I am obsessed with it. Over the years I have worked with numerous landlords and listened to their comments and tidbits of wisdom. Agree or disagree there is something worthwhile to learn from everyone. One guy I did excavation work for and then later helped him with general rental fix up always ignored little things and little expenses. He always said, "I don't care, I don't care, just get er done." He would buy excess materials with no plan to return left over stuff to the store. He demo'd projects without regard to savings or collateral expenses. One of his jobs I helped on was not permitted and we were doing major changes. He had us stack ripped out drywall, studs, toilet, sink, into a pile in the front yard, later he planned to haul it away. I warned him that the construction trash pile was obvious and attracted attention. "I don't care, I don't care," was his mantra.

When the county building inspector pulled up, I quietly left, I wanted no part of what was to come. The inspector posted the property with a red card shutting him down. I think he was unable to work on the project for over a month while he got permits, and it cost a few investment bucks too. "I don't care, I don't care." Bet me, he did then.

I think he was flipping that house, but whether flipping or collecting rent, the bottom line is what is left after paying the bills.

I remember it bothered him that my home was paid off and he was paying on a mortgage. What bothered me that he was loose with his spare change and yet complained he had a mortgage.

For us landlords, paying for handymen, drain cleaners, or wasteful habits may make the difference on whether there is positive cash flow for one year or more. One month extra vacancy or getting caught sneaking in a quick remodel can make several years of negative cash flow. We can't all do our own work, but we can all watch our nickels.

It is no wonder some people are negative on rentals if they don't care enough to make a profit.

I don't care!

You should care

Take the money

It is all about money and time. Time is money, so in the end it is only about money.

We learned right away when we started that we did not have the luxury of making the best choices, many times I made the only choice I could afford. For example, I agreed to rent to people I almost assuredly knew I would be evicting in two or three months. I agreed to let tenants move in if they cleaned and painted themselves. I agreed to let them promise to make repairs. I let people move in when I knew they were in the process of being evicted. I did all the so called wrong things landlords do, and paid a price.

Sometimes the tenants are desperate, sometimes the landlord is too. Having a person wave two or three months cash rent in front of you plus deposit is hard to resist when you are faced with mortgage payments and job responsibilities. Taking the cash is like an addict getting a fix.

To this day when I am turning a rental, I'm thinking, maybe someone will come along and take the place as is. Maybe I will pick up my tools, and go sailing tomorrow.

I pat myself on the back when I am able to keep the daily rent flowing. It is not a game, it never has been. Never the less it feels good when I can manage to switch tenants and only lose one or two weeks rent. Even better when I can pull off a back to back with no lost days.

Daily rent

I tell myself that letting a tenant pay late or move in with a promise to pay later is like loaning money. Then I think, would I loan a complete stranger $500 or $1,500. A person I don't know from Adam.

With rentals I am asked all the time to make that kind of loan. I know it is a paycheck to paycheck world for an awful lot of people. If I refuse to play the game and not rent to anyone that can't come up with two months rent plus a thousand dollar deposit, I may have a unit sit empty for a month. Today, that month is likely to be $1,500, and I would be ahead to throw away the deposit, if it means getting the rent flowing again.

I know, you are thinking waiting for a better heeled tenant will pay off in the end. That is simply not true. A tenant with more cash may not be paying his current landlord, he may be much worse. I choose my tenants for a lot of reasons, not all are their available cash, but it helps. It helps a lot.

It's easy to criticize a decision, but you really must look at the big picture, even then there are lots of variables and guesswork.

I loan my tenants money by allowing late or skipped rent, I know I may never get it back. For me, it's part of being a landlord, I try not to lose sleep over it, but I do. If I get rent every month for a year that is 12/12, if I lose a month it is 11/12. In easy to add numbers suppose the rent is a grand a month or 12k a year, lose a month and it's 11k, or $916 per month. I hate to lose the $83.33 per month but If I switch tenants I may lose twice that in daily rent. The new tenant may be worse. What if the house is only worth $895 per month. In that case I'm actually way ahead. Like I said, I try not to lose sleep over a little rent. I lose sleep over zero rent, so should all landlords in my opinion.

Getting paid

Times certainly change. We have gone from cash is king to plastic to online payments.

We learned right away to get paid. Until money changes hands the deal is not real. After money is received the deal is only as valuable as the amount of money exchanged. This means that $100 deposit to hold it may be all you ever get. The old adage, "shake on it," or "my word is my bond," is pure bunk fast talk for many. In fact we consider conversation about honesty and trust to be red flags. Another big red flag is when people insert god or religion into the discussion. My inner cynic is beginning to glow as I think of all the money we have been promised that never materialized.

We try not to take checks but sometimes we do. The problem with checks is that we make plans today and then in a month or two the plans can come apart because the check is returned. For our vacation rentals we prefer checks because they are sent many months in advance and have time to settle. Credit cards we don't like because they may be disputed months after checks have cleared.

For almost our entire landlording life we have had one tenant or another that has come by our home and paid in cash or I pick it up. It usually starts out cash because of lack of banking, then we just continue it. Linda likes monthly cash drop offs to replenish her spending kitty. Lately, our son that rents from us is her only cash payer. If he switches to PayPal she may run out of lunch money and then I will have to pay.

We tell new monthly tenants to send money orders, or bank checks. Bill paying services are not high on my list for two reasons. First, their envelopes are plain and have no hint they are for rent. I dread I may toss one out with junk mail. Second the tenant goes online to order the rent be sent but by the time it is processed and we receive it, it is late. Of course if the tenant would pay earlier it would not matter, but they don't

Since discovering PayPal we have been pushing people to make payments with them. For our VR houses we suggest guests make their reservation with PayPal, that way they get instant booking and a confirmed date. Then,they send a check for the balance or use PayPal again for the final payment sixty days before their vacation date.

PayPal

Still talking PayPal, we have had a number of issues come up that concern me. Several times we have had transactions disputed and the final outcome was in doubt and took a long time to resolve. Communication is one way, their way, (PayPal) leaving us not knowing what to do. I realize there is nothing we can do. With a local bank, we can walk in and have a meeting with the manager, at least we can talk.

Another concern for us is online security. With several banks, Visa and PayPal, VRBO, and Airbnb interconnected, I think it is possible all our online finances could go south at once due to hacking or simple operator error. For our protection we keep a separate bank account not tied to any other as our back up. In the investing world they call diversification a good thing, in banking I call it a more secure thing.

Late fees

I keep saying, I will improve and update what I do but I never do. All I do is talk. I have become one of those people I say to watch their feet, not listen to their twaddle.

I think that all I need to do is include in my rental agreement two things. One is that I can update the agreement and they must agree to future changes I may mail them. And two, I need to include a line stating their deposit is to be applied to unpaid late fees and any other indebtedness they have incurred, ie. final utilities, missing remotes, even light bulbs add up a bunch. You would be surprised how much you forget until it is too late. I have talked before about watching nickels. Every missing led bulb is forty nickels.

Last thing, I will never consider being my own attorney or being able to write competent effective legalese that will hold up in court. But, BUT, We have never gone to court where our rental agreements were ever discussed or even mentioned. I have been to court way too many times on evictions, in fact for one busy period when I constantly rented to the wrong people, the county court clerks nodded to me when I arrived to file papers. I can think of other things I would rather be recognized for. Being a regular patron of FED court is not one of them.

The take away is that, while the rental agreement is crucial, my day to day, move in and move outs have been 100% defined by back and forth discussion, not by what a judge decrees. If I can show the tenant in writing where they agreed to use their deposit for miscellaneous charges, the argument is settled before it starts.

One last, last thing. Sometimes people think their responsibility is limited to the amount of the deposit. As a practical matter that is true, it is simply not worth the effort to beat them up and still not get paid. However more responsible tenants concerned about their credit and reviews will behave better if they think they are on the hook for more than the deposit amount, so making that clear in the rental agreement is a good idea.

Let's talk more ROI & cash flows

This is an area I did not want to get into because so many bloggers with management PhD's have written volumes. I have no credentials, heck, I don't even like math but I have daily experience with my own money and my own sweat.

I get a kick out of people shopping property for sale and ask how much the mortgage payments are, and then the rent, and then quickly toss out a cash flow amount. Wow pretty healthy they say. My worst performing investment exceeds all the others in cash flow. My best property drags a hundred out of me every month. How can this be, non math wiz's ask. Simple the bad one is paid off, hence high cash flow, the great one is mortgaged to the hilt and is paying its own way, but has nothing left over, no cash flow.

I try to look at a properties true value, this is not so tough if you are honest with your self. I then look at its rental income, with a little division and subtracting any outrageous expenses, you can determine a simple return. I compare income property this way. What should be clear as mountain water is that the more valuable a property is, the more income it should produce. In a perfect system a property worth ten times another ought to produce ten times the other. When looking in my portfolio, (fancy investor talk), I see an under producing expensive castle and some well producing starter homes. Obviously I will trade the castle for a block of starter homes, improving my lot in life.

I ran this little scenario by you because I wanted you to see that it is simple to understand but not so easy to really get on top of, and here is why.

Most of us, and I mean me, can't go out and buy and sell at will. We need down payments, we need gold (remember the golden rule) we need credit scores, financing, time, favorable interest rates, available property to buy. I was able to acquire each of my properties because at the time things came together and I was ready to act. Not because I analyzed my portfolio and snapped my magic fingers.

One last reason I don't do what the PhD's say to do is, I like my castle and I don't want to part with it. You might even say, *I don't care,* if I haven't ruined that phrase. That last statement trumps all other thinking and ultimately delegates this witty charade to the waste basket.

The real non cash flow income

We have found after more than three decades of rental bookkeeping that during many early years some of our houses lost money and that depreciation deductions and long term appreciation were the only justifications for continuing our ownership. Some years a single vacancy or water heater failure takes out the entire years positive cash flow.

Imagine that you are typical and that your rental home throws off virtually zero cash flow. You are in it for the long haul knowing that rents will increase and your property value will go up too. You knew when you bought the house that it would require new exterior paint sometime in the future. The future has caught up to you, in the mail is a letter from your insurance company. They are not renewing your policy due to poor exterior maintenance and peeling paint, they send a picture of a drive by inspection to support their position.

Having a *refused to renew* on your houses insurance record will be costly, making it next to impossible to get quality fair priced insurance. (Remember that box on your insurance application you checked saying you have never been turned down for insurance coverage?) In a panic you call your agent and he/she assures you that if you prove you have painted the house the insurance company will back off and renew you after all.

You get bids of $3000 plus paint and decide to do it yourself. Your insurance is renewed. Now look at your cash flow for that house, it is still zero but you just painted it your self saving you 3K. If you had hired a painter you would be short 3K from your bank account but you are not short are you. So you just made 3K. You paid your self $3,000, you just don't see it in your pocket, but it is in your bank account. If you had paid someone, you sure as heck would have seen and felt that. Now repeat this scenario many times over as a plumber, handyman, property manager, etc. and you will understand how a landlord may hire themselves and make money even though on the books there is no profit or income.

Hiring yourself is a great way to be self employed. Many of our homes were fix up projects first and rentals second. At tax time you may deduct all your materials and expenses just like any contractor you hire but not your personal labor. Your working for free, but the money you pay yourself is not considered income either. Talk to your tax preparer.

Elsewhere in this book I credited Ben Franklin with, *A penny saved is a penny earned,* I also said to watch your nickels. Now you know how to put money in the bank simply by not taking it out.

Rent Income mistakes or not?

Earlier I wrote about the management boo boo of not keeping rent up to market level and how far behind I let some properties become.

As a practical matter, nobody refers to their month to month tenancy as expired and whether they are re upping for another thirty days. It is just assumed by everyone that unless someone gives notice, you will both, landlord/tenant, just keep on going as is. In Oregon when a lease expires or in the absence of a written agreement, tenancy becomes thirty day month to month anyway, so it is easy to just let the years go by without adjusting the rent.

However, when a lease nears its expire date, most landlords and tenants are aware and are thinking about new terms and most of all, the new rent amount. Using leases is a good way to assure that

63

you at renewal time adjust the rent appropriately, where as using month to month tenancy and then letting months become years and then decades is an easy lazy way to become hopelessly behind. I know, I make that boo boo. I don't want to know how much rent I could have received, it's too painful to think about.

Some readers will correctly make the connection between low vacancy rates and low rents. It is an absolute fact that landlords lose daily rent and incur turn around expenses every time tenants move out. Something not to ignore is the extra landlord work involved as well. Just recently, Linda mentioned to me that having a vacant house never comes at a convenient time, never. Unplanned vacancy's have impacted our vacations a few times. Our longest renting tenant has been sixteen years. We have had many tenants stay with us seven years. It is very hard to argue we would have been better off raising rents when I look at the added work higher vacancy brings with it.

Last pragmatic thought, it doesn't matter if you use a lease form or no written agreement at all. When and if the time comes to evict for non payment, you go through the same steps to get your house back.

You may think you will sue the tenant for the remainder of the lease period, but it is probably not going to happen. I just want my property back so I can get my daily rent started again.

Keep in mind, I am simply stating what I do. You should make your own choices. I have read that other states have rules that are different, some very pro tenant. I suspect I wouldn't want to own property in certain states.

Who owns the appliances?

There was a time when I was spending significant time and money fixing and replacing refrigerators, ranges, washers and dryers. dishwashers and disposals. Did I miss any appliances?

Linda and I discussed at length between us and others what would happen if we quit offering appliances in our rental homes. I must point out if you haven't figured it out already, our early years were primarily in lower income areas. I don't know if the economic status made a difference but we found out to our pleasant surprise that we had no trouble renting our places without appliances. We told tenants that if the house had any appliances they could use them but if they needed service or broke they would have to get their own. I removed dishwashers and disposals as they broke. The dishwasher space became a large cabinet, disposals history. We had little to no blow back for this policy, I saved a ton of time and money. Tenants were still heating houses with the oven and clearing ice from freezers with ice picks but we were no longer paying the bill, they were.

My death trap time bomb

Don't ever make a deal you can't take to the grave. Sounds kind of harsh but it is common sense. Unfortunately common sense often gets over ruled by frantic desperate moves. Would you ever buy a house if the bank said, you must make a balloon payment in four days? How about agreeing to financing where the interest rate may be bumped twelve points over six years, but you pay no principle?

The first one I made up, the second one is an agreement I accepted about a dozen years ago and almost bought the farm. In a nutshell we bought two homes, both were 1031 exchanges and we were in a hurry to leave for our vacation in Costa Rica. We were under the gun (45 day rule) and in desperation didn't fully appreciate the loans true risk. *Fully appreciate,* is the lame excuse for where you ignore what you know is true. The financing we took on was a variable rate interest only loan. No principle payment for ten years, interest adjusted every six months. Then the economy tanked, investor **65** money dried up and ten years quickly flew by. Our two rental loans came due and were adjusted, principle became due, and we went from a $800 positive cash flow to losing $200 a month. For the arithmetic challenged, we suddenly had a thousand dollar shortfall in our checking account every month and it was going to be adjusted for the worse every six months.

The urge to bet the farm, bet on your performance, bet on a buyers market, bet on how smart you think you are, is overwhelming. Don't invoke the risk/reward ratio if that's what you are thinking, you are only fooling yourself, leaning on another cliché. The only safe bet is the bet you can afford to lose or take to the grave.

I use the term "death trap," you can call it what you want, but biting off more than you can handle, risking what you have chasing a few more dollars was a dumb way of protecting my families greatest assets.

> *Risk reward ratio*
> *More risk = more reward*
> *Flawed thinking in my opinion*

FYI, the feds saved our rears when they came up with HARP, Home Affordable Refinance Program, we grudgingly converted both loans to 30 year fixed at normal apr's. We managed to get our cash flow (with rent increases) back in the red but no where near what we had been enjoying. In retrospect, what we did worked out fine but I was stressed for years worrying about these two variable rate time bombs.

Risk taking

After talking about the death trap it is easy to think the prudent person should stay out of real estate, not true, just don't take huge risks.

When I talk with other landlords and wannabe landlords, sometimes I hear cliches tossed around and statements I don't agree with. Some are dumb, some are flat out wrong. When we repeat incorrect cliches they earn credibility and become lethal. Using cliches as short cut thinking is in everyday life, but conclusions drawn may be flawed and then we make poor choices.

Some examples: "It takes money to make money" while sometimes true and more so when you employ the golden rule thinking and substitute gold for money, simply saying the cliché suggests you have to spend money and the more the better. The problem begins when you embrace this cliche and let it cloud your decisions. You must be wise, not witty.

Too good to be true

This is a tough one because I have come across deals that really are too good to be true that turned out to be true. The answer is, do a little research, trust your gut, and don't let greed sway your thinking.

Scams are everywhere, the person may not really be who they say they are. I can not direct you how to stay out of trouble, maybe you need to get scammed a few times like us so you develop that cynical outlook that saves your butt.

I will tell you in my experience, the con jobs I fell for I did not see coming, the person fooling me was always very very likable and seemed to be exceedingly honest.

This is my truth and reinforces my rule that we all have the gold and that great deals are simply exchanges of one another's gold. The mistake here is when you start thinking that your time is so valuable that you substitute "Time is money" and then make a rash decision. Which brings up another cliché that goes something like, "A fool and his money are soon parted."

Watch the nickels

"Watch the nickels, the dollars will take care of themselves," is not a common cliché, rather a rule a mentor repeated to me once, and it stuck to this day. Here's an example we experienced recently that cost us over three hundred dollars reinforcing the rule.

We had a vacation rental tenant ask us to authorize a one time sports channel upgrade for the weekend they stayed at our beach place. I ordered the $20 upgrade but then forgot, ignored, simply couldn't be bothered, thought it was smart, it doesn't matter, it was several years before I canceled the upgrade. The bottom line is that I was not watching my nickels and they added up to a heavy sack. I did not follow my mentors advice.

All those monthly little recurring bills are suspect and as your holdings expand so does your potential for loss. Insurance for all our houses is another suspect.

If you take away anything from this book, take away, *Watch the nickels, the dollars will take care of themselves.*

Rent obsession

I hope you have already read my words, daily rent, many times, perhaps I seem obsessed with getting it.

Land lording is a business, and the only income is the rent. If my unit sits empty, I am not earning income. My way may not be the other guys way, but it works for me. Get the daily rent.

Most of the time, word that a rental is empty spreads around the neighborhood pretty fast, neighbors are always watching, not much gets past them. I have to balance my time working on required repairs with talking with prospective tenants.

It is common for an eager new tenant to offer to take the house "as is," in exchange for a break in the deposit or rent. When talking with people that want to rent from me, I try to read them, find out what I can. People are on their best behaviors when they are trying to convince me to rent to them, but they drop hints worth noting. When a person asks how much to move in but does not know or ask the rent, it tells me they are not interested beyond taking possession. I have had my share of tenants that pay all the move in costs and then can't pay the second months rent.

So that brings up the last months rent and deposits. If you let them move in without getting the last months rent, you are cruising for a bruising and probably get stressed every first of the month. With a new tenant, I pay close attention to their rent habits and communications. When the rent is late, I start thinking, that's okay, I have the last months rent. However that means the clock is ticking and I have less than thirty days to get my house back and re-rented or I lose some daily rent.

I treat every tenant different, my mistakes have been many, but most of my mistakes, I saw coming. One might ask, "well if you saw it coming, why did you do it anyway?" For the money of course, is probably the number one answer. In our family landlord business, the big picture is always influencing otherwise simple choices. We need the money was the big picture on a daily basis for years. In retrospect, what is wrong with succeeding? Well?

Rent increases

I have said before, I am not telling you what to do, I am telling you what I have done, and some of the results.

I read once in a book on rental management by a cpa/bookkeeper that the biggest mistake he sees people make is not keeping the rents current with the market. He was speaking right to me, I am guilty as charged. I remember lowering the rent to help a couple stay another six months. There was a time in our career when rents were climbing fast and we actually joked about looking forward to tenants moving out so we could raise the rent in multi hundred dollar increments.

I will recount some situations. First, we had a tenant for over sixteen years. When I finally got around to checking the rent appropriateness you can imagine how far off we were. I did not want to hit the family with a terrific financial shock and yet I did want to make a fair adjustment. I did my homework and came up with a number for their rent that was still about 10% low. I sent the tenant a letter explaining my calculations and said I would phase in the increases over ten months.

Next rent boo boo was a condo we still own. We let the rents get behind again, and again I phased the increases. However this time I phased it over three months because I was secretly hoping they would move out. They did not.

In our heyday if you can call it that, we owned sixteen units and management was becoming more than we enjoyed. I remember a cash crunch hit our family. More kids more monthly bills, something like that. I across the board raised rents fifty dollars and brought in $800 more each month and solved our income shortage almost overnight.

Some truism's to reflect on: Experts that don't own anything will tell you that you must maximize rent and minimize expense. That's too obvious to discuss, but if rent sky rockets beyond their budgets, at some point your tenants will move out, and new tenants will become priced out, your vacancy rate climbs, your cash (daily rent) plummets, and your return is lower. However making a rent boo boo like us is no way to run a business either. High occupancy comes at a cost So does high vacancy.

I don't think there is a fix or formula for this dilemma, rent is a balancing act. I think everyone must apply their own big picture and make it work for them.

Who pays the garbage bill

Portland requires the property owner to pay the garbage bill and be on account. They wont work with renters. They also require all properties to have garbage service, promising to recycle everything is not sufficient. They eventually lightened up a little allowing long term lessees to be on garbage accounts.

When we started, garbage could be quite messy. Often when a tenant falls behind on rent they are already cutoff from utilities. It was not unusual to get a house back with no electricity, water and mountains of garbage overflowing all over the yard.

When the city required landlords pay for garbage service, bad tenants could still take out the garbage even if everything else was shut off. I think the law worked but at landlord expense, not tenant expense where it belongs.

Trash disposal is outrageously expensive, and a vacant house is an easy target. We have on numerous occasions had trash dumped on our properties. Not surprisingly, it is a problem primarily in lower rent areas. A house with a driveway that goes alongside the house affords almost complete privacy for someone illegally dumping out the back of a pick up truck. Persons will advertise junk hauling, charge people to haul away trash, and then dump it at a vacant house.

We were caught by surprise one time when we discovered our tenant had been making his living by hauling junk and had filled the entire back yard of his own place with trash. I think it took two forty foot container loads and several days work to haul it all off.

Something I learned when looking at places for sale was to be suspicious of mounds in the yard, some call them berms. When you find a berm in an odd place, you guessed it, buried treasure.

Rent competition at vacation rentals

When all the apartments look the same it is a safe bet they will rent for the same amount. The same is true for condo's and houses. In a given area three bedroom homes bring in about the same rent, ditto four bedrooms. When we decided to get into vacation rentals, we found out that the competition was much stiffer than month to month rentals. A cabin that sleeps 12 wouldn't rent if a cheaper one that also slept 12 was available. The only way to get more rent was to have more and better amenities like a hot tub or pool table. I can't tell you if hot tubs pay off, we never had one because of the 24/7 maintenance requirement. Our local help was never dependable and we never hired a management company.

For month to month houses we found that the number of bedrooms is a huge deciding factor but location is still crucial. Even in a so called bad area there are parts that are worse yet. So the next street over might rent well but crack alley may only bring half price and then only from sketchy tenants as well.

We experimented with rents in our VR's and month to month houses. We found as expected that as the rent went up, the takers went down. One would surmise that the quality of tenant/guest would vary with how much they spent, not true for us. Of course our non scientific sample was small. Our experience was that we could hurt our profit by raising the rent too high, and it was not offset by better tenants/guests.   Some of our worst experiences have been with high end high maintenance people and our best have been with those that struggled to pay and asked little in return.

I am eager to negotiate deals if it means lower vacancy. At our VR's I will give away extra weekdays that would be empty anyway. Weekends are the gold for VR's. Our best year ever, was when we rented 52 weekends in a row. For our month to month rentals, I may offer reduced rent for three to six months if it means getting a tenant I want versus letting a house sit empty. Lower vacancy almost always makes up for slightly lower rent. Having tenants stay for five years is so much better for the bottom line than one year, believe me. Less work as well.

Rooming houses

This subject rarely comes up, I don't know why not, we have
72   done it three times. For us, our so called boarding houses have

been four and five bedroom homes that we rented individual bedrooms. Each tenant paid rent for their bedroom and shared the house. When a tenant moved out we would have an empty bedroom, not an empty house.

Our first rooming house was an older remodeled home we bought from the Oregon Department of Veteran Affairs. The property had a stand alone garage on a smallish corner lot. Interestingly, all five of the bedrooms already had deadbolts, I simply re keyed them.

We had three males and two females most of the time. We enlisted one of the guys to be manager, his pay was to have the best room with a bathroom. We also rented the garage as a storage only building, so we in essence had six low end rentals. Our combined rent was much more than the house could rent for as a single family home.

The system at this house only worked so so, we did hear complaints from the girls about some of the guys, and subsequent high turn over cut into the bottom line. Since the lot was a corner property we had adequate parking without irritating the neighbors too much.

All in all it was not worth it to us to run a rooming house at that location and we eventually rented to a family. That family stayed for over fifteen years until we sold the property. Keeping the rent very low contributed to the long occupancy, but the tenant almost never contacted us for any reason which also affected us not raising the rent as often as we might have.

Our next rooming house was near a local college that needed off campus housing. We did not intentionally start as a rooming house but rented the five bedroom house to a group of five students that came to us. We made each tenant responsible for the rent, explaining to them that if one couldn't/wouldn't pay, the others were still on the hook for the entire rent.

In writing this book I recall very few problems or issues with the arrangement. I remember running CAT 5 wires on the outside siding to every bedroom plus the main living room, boy was that ugly. It was also easy to rip off when I got it ready to sell nine years later.

An issue that is true anytime you have a house full of young adults is immature actions and lack of personal responsibility. Many of the students were law students but that didn't stop them from writing detailed treatise on walls and burning a sofa in the back yard at midnight.

Our third rooming house, we still own. It has four bedrooms and again was not intended to be a rooming house but a house full of young friends with one in charge to pay the rent. Each tenant is responsible for the entire rent they figure it out among themselves and only one pays the rent. We handle the utilities and tack it onto the rent. It has been over five years now and none of the original group is still around. Once again, as people move out, the remainders find replacements and tell me later.

It is obvious that young people are not the best custodians, the house is taking a slow steady thumping. However it is primarily cosmetic and filthy, not destroyed. I can fix it better than ever when the time comes. In the meantime I'm getting good steady rent, the police and neighbors don't call. I'm a happy landlord.

I would not recommend our rooming house system to anyone that gets emotional or upset when their house is abused, it may be hard to take, but it has worked well for us.

.

I would definitely recommend roommate rentals for someone living in the house as owner/manager, that would change everything. In fact I think a young single person could make a very healthy income this way and in a short time purchase more, expanding into an empire. Home sharing could easily be the new wave, it may already be here.

My methods are mine alone

Okay, some of you will want to skip this page. I say that because what I do is not what experts say to do.

First some back story. Our first homes were in rough parts of town. Gun shots after dark were becoming common, but not so much in the day time. Unemployment was the norm and welfare moms were the only ones with a steady income. Later, we bought homes in a better area known affectionately as felony flats where blue collar people lived and worked. Eventually we picked up and traded into homes in the burbs and vacation homes on the coast and Mt Hood.

My goals have always been to pay the mortgage and make a living, much like everyone I suppose, but I also want to avoid fights and minimize my work. When you have a beat up house in a bad part of town, your tenant pickings are slim. Choice number one may be a single mom with kids receiving aid from the church and a part time job she is lying about. She has $500 cash, the rent is $375. Choice number two is a couple with jobs but wont have money until they get paid in two weeks or their current landlord refunds their deposit. Choice number three has first and last months rent and a $250 deposit and drives a nice car but has no references, job or current landlord.

I take number three. The daily rent is all I have coming and they have sixty days worth. I give them the keys and agree to start the rent asap. I have talks with my tenant during our initial meeting, I look them in the eye for emphasis, if they talk street talk, I may talk a little coarse myself. I tell them if they are late with the rent, I will give them a 72 hour notice to begin eviction proceedings. I ask them if they know how an eviction works. I explain that the sheriff will get them out of the house by the time their last months rent is gone. In short, I tell them not to mess with me or they will be gone.

Please understand, I was intentionally being a bad ass back then, I wanted the tenants to fear the consequences of not paying their rent.

My methods

Reading my three choices you may think choice number two was best because they appeared normal, had jobs and a **75** landlord. You are probably right but in my thinking, they are not serious or they are not any good because they had no money and offered nothing. I take the money guaranteeing me two months rent. My choice (number three) demonstrated responsibility by having all the money, a car and was ready to move in. Not having a landlord reference or job is not all that unheard of in an area with high unemployment and a varied underground economy.

Some landlords will prorate the rent if it is in the middle of the month as they should but I require first and last plus the deposit no matter when the move in date. I still prorate, but I calculate the prorate for the part month and have them pay that amount for their second months rent. Doing it this way means I always get two months rent for sure at move in, even if things go bad. It means my rental pays its own way for two months. It's all about money, the daily rent.

Get the money. In my life as a contractor and landlord I have had numerous opportunities to turn down money that is owed to me. Why would I do that? I hear associates say, "I'll send you a bill," or "mail me a check." In my family we have a saying, "Never turn down money," Granted, there are times when I do turn down money, dumb deals and criminal activities are exempted. I mean in every day dealings. Talk to any business that carry's accounts or small contractor and they will tell you that getting paid is an important part of their business.

When my customer or tenant pulls out a check or cash and I don't have my paperwork ready, I say, "yes, give it to me. I will mail you a paid invoice later." *Never turn down money*, my kids still joke about it today. More later.

Never turn down money

Chapter 4

Landlord Mistakes

~~Nine~~ _Ten_ *major mistakes*

Making mistakes has been said to be the fastest education one may acquire. Or was it the most expensive way to learn? I think both are true. Another saying is, *learning the hard way* .

Lets not equate mistakes or hard knocks with free education. Far from free, the cost of mistakes puts investors out of business, sometimes losing their entire investment or more.

> ### *Smart landlords expect the unexpected*

I have listed mistakes in no particular order of importance, they are all important.

Mistake #1 - letting emotions rule the day

Experts teaching, *how to get rich in real estate,* will tell you not to be emotionally attached to your investment property because it will cause you to make poor decisions. I have owned, bought and sold all sorts or property. Some I really really liked, some not so much, and one fell out of favor over time until I hated it. Emotional involvement? heck yes, cloud my thinking? I certainly hope so. Did I make proper decisions and choices? Yes. How is that possible when the experts say otherwise.

Everything we do involves emotions, If I took my personal feelings out of my many real estate decisions I would possibly have more money, possibly less, but I would definitely be second guessing myself and constantly worried that I made the right choice. **77**

I think rephrasing the entire emotional involvement conundrum and calling it *pragmatic thinking* is a better choice. In my way of thinking, I buy, sell, fix, trade or keep something because it furthers my big plan, not because it brings me the best return. If I turn down a very good offer because I am emotionally attached to some old place or my children beg me to keep it, that's fine also. That does not mean I endorse unrealistic wishful thinking as a way to run things, far from it. That would be the end of everything including the big plan.

What I'm saying is that emotions need not be denied or allowed to run the show, they need to be acknowledged and acted upon pragmatically so you arrive at the planned destination.

Mistake #2 - not having a long term (big) plan

My plan in the seventies was to buy a bunch of houses and retire. I guess I succeeded, except it has been over three decades. In retrospect, my plan was pretty bare and basic. I wish I would have had three mentors. Someone to teach and convince me about good leverage which would have made me fabulously wealthy early on. Someone to mentor me about landlording. I don't mean the basic rental management 101 stuff. I mean what's in my book, the real everyday stuff. And someone to clue me in about middle age and latter years before they got to me.

Some readers probably thought I was going to outline a plan, I just did.

Mistake #3 - placing bets on the future

Lets clarify, we all bet on the future. What I mean is bets we can't afford to lose. Few stock market investors consider margin calls good news and stay away from that kind of investing. They think it is gambling or speculation and I concur. When a rental water heater needs immediate replacement it is a landlord margin call and can not be ignored. A dead furnace in the dead of winter, a much bigger margin call. So landlords are betting on the future, albeit a much less volatile future than the stock market, that is for sure. I protect myself and hedge my bets by having a few extra bucks operating capitol and easy readily available credit. A Visa or Master card with a $25,000 limit and no or very low balance is smart in my opinion. In all our years we have never needed more than a grand or so of emergency money but a high credit limit raises your FICO score which should lower your insurance, so why not.

Mistake #4 - under or over estimating and unrealistic expectations

I think this mistake is in my dna. When I want something I routinely ignore or discount advice and in my head, paint everything rosy to convince myself I am doing the right thing. Linda says I underestimate by one third all repair jobs. I know I overestimate how much rent increase a remodel job will bring. Being unrealistic is easy to fix, simply ask someone else what they think of your idea. Of course that runs the risk of them telling you what you don't want to hear.

Mistake #5 - not counting nickels and dimes

An older friend, mentor if you will, said a very simple thing to me when we started out buying rentals. He said, "watch your nickels and dimes, the dollars will take care of themselves." He was so right, I have seen the proof in my dealings many times and in my daily life. It is unlikely I will misplace or waste a thousand dollars, but I dribble nickels like I have holes in all my pockets. I see others doing the same thing. Guess what, it adds up big time and is so easy to correct. I wont say make a list or score card or your expenses like some advice columnist. Just pay attention and quit wasting money. If you really need to have a trick in your bag, take your credit cards out of your reach and pay cash for everything including gas - no exceptions. Shut off your online buying too. Other than the online part, it is the way I try to operate today.

Don't take this concept too far and then blame me if you become known as a stingy curmudgeon. That's your problem.

Mistake #6 - developing tunnel vision

A defender of acute tunnel vision will use words like focus and goal oriented. I say things like making mistakes and missing opportunities. Working towards your goal or big picture is fine but ruining your marriage should not be in the cards. Chasing dollars is great, but not in exchange for missing your kids growing up. There is a cure for tunnel vision and putting off the cure is proof of what ails you. Making time for yourself and family is not that hard.

Mistake #7 - paying too much

This seems like a no-brainer but it's not. In the excitement of choosing an investment property it is all too easy to make mistake #4. Over and under estimating rears its ugly head. Making an offer is when you need a clear head for numbers. If you are going to keep a property for a long time it must pay its way. Buying any old thing hoping inflation and appreciation will float all boats is nonsense, it must bring in the rent. A rent comparison analysis is a must if you expect rental income. A simple craigslist search will do but it must be done before your offer.

If the plan is to sell the property in a year or so it does not need to be a bread winner, instead it needs guaranteed appreciation. If the market flattens and you made a mistake buying on a wish and a hope, you must stick it out and make it a long term rental. Otherwise you failed.

There is no formula, what may seem to be a good deal in a buyers market may make you wish you'd stay home two months after you close on it. I'm not a fan of buying and playing the appreciation game, it requires too much thinking and is speculative gambling. I get the rent, and make low offers.

80

Mistake #8 - not understanding liquidity

This a two edged sword, you can't jump in and out of real estate like a mutual fund or online day trading account. Thirty to sixty days is the very best you can hope for after you make a move. If you are selling and expecting the proceeds to save your butt, you may as well kiss it goodbye or have a back up plan. When a cyclical market nose dives, sales dry up. All markets are cyclical.

On the other hand an illiquid investment such as real property may save your rear because it slows to a crawl almost all dealings helping to negate dumb moves and rash decisions. Plus that mortgage principle payment is a forced savings account with regular deposits. In my family that's almost our entire savings, illiquid or not.

Mistake #9 - listening to others

After reading my thoughts about mentoring, one would think I am about to contradict myself. No, I listen to everyone but I do my own thinking and make my own decisions.

I have talked about lazy thinking probably too much, maybe it (lazy thinking) should be listed as mistake number ten. Lazy thinking is where someone absorbs diatribe from others as the gospel without question. They think people don't lie or have an agenda, they defer to so called experts, they hear things on the news. Lazy thinkers are being force fed information that might not be accurate. It's what we all do, it is what salesmen and advertisers develop into an art. For proof, just listen to any radio or TV broadcast of news or advertising. Listen with a critical ear for manipulative words or pushing the audience one way or the other. I think if you do you will come away with a realization that you must filter out the garbage and draw your own conclusions. Not be a lazy thinker gobbling up everything.

Mistake #10 abusing leverage

.

This is real simple, it means borrowing too much and then getting in trouble because your ship never makes port or actually sinks leaving you unable to pay the bills. Fortunately mortgage company's have some basic qualification rules they enforce so it is hard to borrow too much on a rental. The problem is the credit cards that are passed out like candy. Number one, they have very high rates. Number two I have one in my wallet. Number three, I say, it's okay I'll pay it off except I don't. Number four, some things in the landlord business can't wait until later. Number five, see numbers one to four.

Today we deal primarily in cash. Even for our day to day repairs and running around money. Using cash helps us a lot with not running up the cards. Cash is inconvenient but it works. I know lots of people today are cash-less. They must either keep careful track of credit purchases so they don't dig a hole or have more than adequate capital backing them so they can charge freely.

I set up my bank account to automatically pay off my monthly credit card purchases. This way I don't pay interest on my credit card but I still try not to use it and pay cash when ever I can, even for gas in my car. My kids use direct deposit for their pay checks and say it is too much trouble to go to the bank to get cash. I go to the extra trouble, I know it is my best way of staying out of credit trouble.

It's okay to be a dinosaur.
A mentor once told me he was a dinosaur, an almost extinct species left over from depression days when cash was king.

Rent Mistakes

Making mistakes is part of landlording, but they can be corrected and the sooner the better.

I'm not talking about mixing the wrong paint color. I'm talking about the wrong tenant or wrong house, major mistakes. When I have goofed and rented to a bad tenant, I have either known it and accepted the outcome which has been most cases, or almost immediately regretted it. The answer is to get rid of them at minimal cost and disruption. Just about every time it is a non payment rent issue. If I fall for their excuses, I prolong the inevitable, I learned to be very hard nosed and issue a 72 hour notice on day number eight. In Oregon you are not allowed to give notice in the first seven days, a built in grace period that resets every month. You can yell and complain on day one, but legal notice is on day eight. After giving proper notice, If they don't comply 100% you may at your discretion file papers to get them out. In essence you are declaring your rental agreement done with (null and void). You don't have to accept partial payment or some impossible promise. The problem I usually have is I am constantly weighing the cost of flipping the tenant versus taking what ever deal is offered and kicking the can down the road. My choice is mostly determined by my big picture, other vacancy's, other jobs to do, upcoming planned vacations, etc. I will make allowances and cut a deal to let them stay longer if it buys me time to get things in order. The take away though is that I try to get rid of a mistake asap, not let it aggravate me for six months and then toss them anyway.

The wrong house is much more difficult to correct and may take a long time and/or cost a bundle. Or worse, it may not sell and I am forced to rent it to pay bills making it that much harder to sell. A real catch 22 may develop.

The money pit or constant fixer is one type of wrong house that I can usually deal with. It's the expensive home that does not make enough rent that is my real thorn.

We bought lots of money pits, you read correctly. In the beginning we did not have much choice, we bought what we could, not what we wanted. Run down money pits in bad parts of town became our homes away from home. Felony flats, crack alley, drive by shootings and bullet riddled doors and walls are not what anyone should want to be involved with but it is how we started. No it does not build character, it fuels cynicism and hypertension.

Money Pit Mistakes

Again I have the urge to warn readers, what we have done is not for everyone, it's simply what we have done and made work for us. Perhaps our colorful history will help some aspiring landlords chart their own better course and avoid a few of the many rocks we hit.

We bought our money pits with our eyes wide open, it was no surprise things were falling apart or that our tenants weren't stellar citizens. On the other hand, our tenants tended to not demand much and accepted crappy conditions as normal. Owning slummy property does not make one a slumlord. Ignoring your responsibilities, not respecting your tenants, cheating your tenants define slumlords.

Selling problem property might be the best way to correct the original mistake, however not making a profit buying and selling or worse, losing, is really hard to stomach and leaves the stigma that you are not very smart.

We swallowed our pride one time giving away a mistake property. We walked away with nothing, six months work and thousands of dollars, all gone. Bailing out was the correct choice, I have never regretted it or looked back.

Selling on contract works well. As seller you have something someone out there wants, after all you were once the buyer. With a contract, anything you and the buyer may agree to can be reduced to writing and you have a deal. In my way of thinking, my goal is to find someone I trust that will take over my responsibilities and pay me regularly. Someone just like me would be perfect.

We have sold on contract, or relinquished day to day management is a better way to describe it, five times on four homes. One we took back. Each deal is a little different, two have had no down payment. I am looking forward to making more contract deals. The downside is that we are not receiving any big lumps of cash. The upside is we are increasing our monthly income while freeing up our time. I think people overlook making contract deals. Being the banker feels right. Real estate agents certainly don't talk about them because there is little if any commission available. I have detailed our contract deals in another chapter.

Way too valuable home mistake

The expensive home mistake is when I buy a house that is worth more than it will rent for. Some people in my own family don't get this simple principal. ROI - return on investment. It doesn't matter if a property has massive cash flow if it doesn't have income commensurate to its value. Expensive homes have amenities people pay for as owners but renters draw the line at fair market value.

This mistake happened to us when we got a fantastic deal in a rising market. Linda and I jumped on it with four feet. We had done two exchanges and had a wheelbarrow full of money that needed a new home. We made a low all cash offer with no inspections. Boom, just like that we owned a classy split level, large lot, big shop in a desirable neighborhood. I would love to have lived there.

We sanded and satin sheened the solid oak floors, touched up the paint and discussed the rent we would get. Not near enough, It became painfully clear that our return was not going to be anywhere near what our less affluent homes brought in. The home was too nice, too expensive, too desirable, too valuable. With the rising market the situation was getting worse every day.

We shifted gears and sold it, that's right I became a very non landlordly flipper. We then traded our new bigger bucket of cash for two less expensive places and got much more rent and a better ROI.

A decidedly non landlord thought is, why didn't we keep flipping in the rising market? No comment, except perhaps that is why I don't need to work anymore.

This next thought seems like crazy logic but hear me out and it will make sense. If rent holds up, during a falling market, rentals become better and better to own.   I joked half seriously with my realtor one day that my house he had listed was not selling even after we lowered the price over two hundred thousand dollars when the 2009 crash hit. The rent stayed the same, the more the homes value fell, the better my ROI. I finally pulled the listing and signed a ten year triple net lease deal with an escalation formula. It's true, the house became pretty much useless to sell but a great rental. Do the math. When I do the ROI calculation for this house I am using the current market value of the home as my investment not the cash I have into the house.

Time wasting managers

I am referring to landlords and wannbe's that are always asking others what to do, which is totally okay, but they don't take basic simple advice. I understand they see their own big picture but sometimes the clear choice is so clear it is maddening that they are wasting your time, my time, their time, everybody's time and they still make dumb decisions.

Worse are the lazy managers that abdicate, not delegate, their responsibilities, end up with bad results and then blame the outcome on others instead of wising up, learning from the experience and doing better in the future. These are the ones that lose money and then bad mouth the rental business.

Why do I care what these people say and do, easy, landlording is my chosen profession, my passion, it is what I do and I am proud of my diminutive empire and apparent life work. Consequentially I don't have much patience for screw ups and easy-money-flippers passing themselves off as landlords. (Boy, what set me off?)

Rental Scams

It can't happen to me, oh yes it can. When someone gives you a check knowing that it will be returned and you accept it instead of tossing them out on their tea kettle, you have been scammed. A minor scam that sets you back a week or two but you fell for it when you took the check. If that is the worse that ever happens count your blessings.

We had a house, Sam's house in fact. It was vacant and we were working there everyday making it perfect. The summer weather was great, we were dolling up the yard. I was mowing and edging the lawn. The roses were already blooming. Linda was pruning. We had for rent signs down on the corner and a steady stream of lookers.

We started talking to a couple that walked up, they were nice, the type I would rent to. They said they had rented the house last night and were just coming by for another look at their new home.

The silence was deafening as Linda and I looked at each other. Linda said, no one had rented the house, we hadn't made a decision yet. They explained they had paid a deposit and first and last months rent to a nice guy around 6 pm. They had walked through the house, he said he was the owner.

Those folks were scammed in an all to common scam. There may have been others but we didn't hear of any. Phoney for rent scams on craigslist are another. All it takes is an empty house, neighbors that

Naive thinking

Thinking I can make any property work out.
Reality: No I can't, nor should you or I want to.

I think most people do a simple analysis before buying a rental, I know we do. We take a wild guess at how much rent we will get, subtract our expected expenses, what ever is left is the profit or POSITIVE CASH FLOW and based on that simple math we decide if we can make a few bucks. Throwing a dart at a map while blindfolded works too and is just as useless.

In our early learning years with many tenants and houses, we figured if we got $100 per month positive cash flow we would buy the house, do the deal, and we would be happy. We were naïve, the actual results for us was that we lost $100 per month. That was a $200 mistake per month on a house that rented for less than $500. In today's market, optimistic analysis on a $1,500 rental is likely to be a $600 monthly mistake. Save time, throw darts.

> Save your optimism for
> weather forecasting

I believe it is human nature to be optimistic, but take it easy when you forecast expenses and income in order to make a rational purchase decision.   You must be capable of absorbing your overly enthusiastic optimism. Lets not gloss over the statement I just made. To be clear you must be able to put in a $1,500 water heater with no notice, you must be able to repair a furnace in the dead of winter for $4,500. You must be able to make your monthly payment obligation when your tenant quits paying rent without warning. The list of *you must's* is long.

As the years piled up we got better at everything, especially mitigating costly mistakes cheaply.

More naive thinking

Reality check: Maybe you can make it work, maybe you can't, but when the rent flow ends, you can't not pay the mortgage.

My handyman income was not sufficient to pay ten plus mortgages let alone one. When a tenant moved out or I evicted them, the clock had already been running since the last rent failed to come in. Every single day is a race to get the rent flowing again. The landlord does not make money collecting deposits or last months rent. The landlords only income is the daily rent. It is imperative to get a nonpaying tenant out of the house asap and the new paying tenant in place. This is not the time for compassion or unfortunately going on vacation.

At the end of the year or five years, when ever you add up your income and look at your performance as a manager, your vacant days impact the bottom line big time. As a manager you have many opportunities to make less money, even lose money, but the only way to make more money is to increase rent or reduce expenses, both you should be doing anyway. As far as raising rent, of course you should stay competitive, but gouging tenants will only get you a few short term dollars at the risk of higher vacancy. Lowering your vacancy rate and reducing expenses is the smart way to maximize your return on investment.

You don't have to be a penny pinching scrooge to be a successful landlord, I'm not and I have done just fine, but I understand vacancy and I understand how gold plated expensive improvements can knock the heck out of the bottom line.

Love it or lose it

When I talk to people that have tried owning rentals I hear a recurring theme. They can't stand renters, then after awhile they lighten up and say they can't stand that they (renters) destroyed their house.

With some quizzing I find out the house in question was their personal residence that they kept as a rental after moving up to a bigger better and much more expensive home in a gated community with restrictive ccr's and required landscape maintenance contracts.

There is nothing wrong with owning and living in a showroom perfect mansion, but a renter will never match or even come close to those standards, why would they, it's not their house. I will bet that these same people drove by their ex home to check up on after they rented it out. That is is recipe for disappointment.

I believe most personal homes make poor rentals unless they were starter homes to begin with. Even so called starters can be so dolled up with granite counters and fancy appliances that the transition to a rental is devastating dollar wise.

As a landlord, I try to shut out my personal feelings for my property, but I have never converted my family home to a rental so I don't have any personal and family memories digging at me. I take a pragmatic view of rentals. When I consider buying a home I am looking at it as a landlord, I will never live there. I look for the rent it will demand and the maintenance issues it will have. I try to spot negatives and not be wowed by emotional candy coatings like thick carpet, Italian marble and backyard fountains and hot tubs. They may look great and add first impression value but I discount the extras as something I will probably have to maintain or replace. In my humble opinion, glitzy baubles don't increase the rent.

Houses with a little glitter will show better and when it is time to sell will bring more but as a rental, I don't see it that way. It is a tough choice, rent versus flip. I think a smart plan is to trade into better rentals not better personal homes unless you are planning to flip soon in which case letting the home sit empty while you market it may be the best action plan.

My intention here was not to disparage or shoe horn renters into the same box, it is simply a fact that owners love their homes and renters are temporary visitors. Except we had a renter family for over sixteen years. I can't really label them as temporary, they were an exception.

Unrealistic expectations

We may separate the real landlord from the chaff here.

When I talk with people that own investment property, I often hear a quick horror story. The stories ring the same. Probably number one is, the renter trashed the place, next they owed six months rent, followed by it took them six months to get the renter out. And then, how they spent five thousand dollars to restore the house to its former glory.

I have lamented before how I fix a place up, it looks and smells great, I rent it, and then I get it back and start over again. I understand this, but I have landlord mentality. I know the paint takes a beating. Vinyl and carpet have limited life's. Decks wear out, and children are rough on fancy trim and brocaded ceilings.

I know some new landlords buy a home for themselves and rent out the old one. They have emotional attachments with the old place and it hurts to see their memories disrespected one upset wannabe told me.

I rented and managed my mothers home for her, my childhood home. It annoyed me when I found graffiti on the walls of my old bedroom. I got over it.

If you can't stand at arms length from your rentals, you can't make smart decisions. You will install gold plated faucets and feel horrible when the Italian marble is cracked. You might also become unhappy with a dismal return on investment if you insist on the best of everything.

I am sure to get some dissenting opinions from people that only rent to the cream of the tenant pool and never have any of the issues I have dealt with. I wish them only the best and their daily rent.

Lets talk con jobs

I'll try to hit just the good stuff. Both units of our up down duplex were empty, so I am sweating not getting my daily rent. I arranged to meet with Troy one afternoon to see the upstairs three bedroom rental.

He was dressed in scrubs, he was on break from the near by hospital. I checked him out as best I could, the hospital wanted my verification request in writing so that was a dead end. His current landlord said good things on the phone. I got the first and last months rent plus deposit from Troy in cash and gave him the keys.

That was the only and last time I saw Troy.

A month later, Troy's phone is dead, and I'm banging on the upstairs door of my duplex.

"Who is it," is the muffled response to my knocking.

"I'm the landlord, I'm looking for Troy." The door opens six inches, far enough for me to see that the fellow inside has to duck to see out the door.

"He ain't here, what do you want," says a truly scary dude. I explain about the rent, the door shuts. Twenty seconds later the door opens and he thrusts me a stack of 20's and 100's. I quickly count it, it's all there.

"Remember Troy," I say to Linda when I get home, "he's gone."

About a month later the police accidentally chased off the drug dealers while looking for someone that used to live there. I suddenly got the place back. It was empty and clean except for a single chair and portable TV with a bent coat hanger antenna, They never intended to live there. I kept the last months rent and deposit. The police didn't arrest anyone, but they tossed out one person for loitering and shut down a drug house business that had more customers than the corner grocery. Apparently Troy doesn't exist.

So lets see where I went wrong. Well everywhere. I was desperate to get my daily rent flowing, I fell for someone that was too good to be true. I liked Troy a lot. I found out later that the phone number I called was a pay phone outside a tavern. I also found out that the drug group I rented to routinely moved every thirty to forty five days, so the police never had much affect. Financially I did very good and re-rented in a few days.

Garage storage fiasco

The rent came in for a while and then it stopped. All I had was a phone number. Worse yet, I had no idea where I stood in the tenant landlord relationship legally. Was I supposed to give seventy two hours notice and file an FED at the courthouse for a storage building.

I went to the property and peered through the single dinghy spider web covered window. I could see the garage building was full of household belongings. While I was there a local thrift store donation pickup and delivery truck backed into the driveway in front of the closed twin roll up doors, two men appeared.

"Hi guys, I'm looking for Bob," I said. We talked, the garage doors stayed closed as did the truck door. Soon I was asking about the late rent. One of the guys piped up that he had paid the rent to Bob, the landlord. I corrected him that I was the landlord and I rented the building to Bob. It became apparent that Bob had subletted the garage to this guy and was absconding with the rent rather than paying me.

I explained to these unfortunate men that they were apparently being cheated by Bob and that they had no claim to my garage. I told them to either pay the rent (again) or get their stuff off my property.

Some time went by, weeks a month I don't remember, but I never saw Bob or the truck drivers again. All the stored household goods remained in my garage, for all I know they abandoned everything.

I still did not know where I stood legally, but I needed my garage empty or some rent and decided I must safeguard what may or may not be abandoned property. I hired two helpers. While moving everything I noticed quite a bit of valuable items, one in particular was an ornate carved wood, air powered pipe organ. It had two large pedals the organist pumped with their feet while playing the keys, and it still worked. There were tools and lots of furniture and appliances. I hauled all of it a few miles to my four-plex basement storage area, locked it up and never looked at it again.

The rest of the story

I can't leave the story unfinished, so I will jump ahead. The four-plex had become a horrible investment, I was in way over my head so to speak. The problems were horrific, including the gang murder of my manager Dave. Several times as I was driving to the plex to fix something or another. I would feel my heart pounding, I would loose my nerve and simply turn around and drive home. Linda would say, "Your back soon," I would explain I got all jittery, I was worried for my safety, health, whatever, I'll go tomorrow I would say.

Soon I ran an ad in the Oregonian newspaper. "Four–plex for sale, $1,000 and take over payments, First person with cash gets it."

I met my buyer one time, the same day the paper came out, I handed him a string of keys and took the grand in cash. I signed a quit claim and told him where to make payments. I explained the storage situation and said it was his to deal with. I was done. My sense of relief when I walked away was undeniable.

Maybe a year or two went by, I happened to talk with the bank representative that held the mortgage for the plex. He was still a little pissed off at me, but so was I at him. He said, "remember that white guy you dumped the plex on," "yeah I said", he said "he turned out to be a huge crack dealer."

Back to the storage story: If you are a detective novel fan, you should have a good theory, I certainly do.

I think Bob and the guys with the thrift store truck were in it together and they lied that they had paid Bob the rent. I think they were real employees of a not for profit charity and the truck was legitimate, but they were stealing donations. My garage was full of stolen property that should have been delivered to the thrift store.

What I don't understand is why or how the state's attorney office got involved. The DA wrote me a letter asking about the stored goods, I told them what I knew including addresses. It has been more than twenty years. I have driven by the four-plex a few times and wondered what would have been in the cards if I had not bailed. The house with the storage garage, I sold on contract, there's still over twenty more years income expected.

> Everyone has their limit,
> landlording may test yours.

Never turn down money

While writing the last essay I remembered a rule I have said many times, mostly to my children. It all started one day when a tenant came by our house to pay rent, but I wasn't home. My daughter or maybe a son told the tenant to come back another time. When I heard about the exchange I said, "WHAT," Followed by, "NEVER TURN DOWN MONEY."

95

It didn't really mean anything at the time except I thought they (my children) could accept rent. It was probably cash, they could write a receipt but that is beside the point. Around that time I worked many jobs with a landscape contractor. I remember his customers would pull out the checkbook to pay him or his employee, but they wouldn't have an invoice or know the amount and would say, we will bill you later.

Here's my point, later on this same contractor was constantly having cash problems because everyone owed him money. He was unable to pay bills, including me. Maybe he should've learned to *never turn down money.*

> *"Never turn down money"*
> (worth repeating)

How to spot mistakes

You have probably heard about the old time carpenters that had no use for levels or squares, they just stood back fifty feet and looked between outstretched parallel hands and pronounced the wall straight. There is some truth to those stories because they did build quality homes, many that are still standing today.

I have spent long hours, some of my readers have too, slaving over a project only to see a huge mistake when I stood back and really looked at what I was doing.

Once when I pulled onto a new home building site I was still in my truck when I spotted a wall that was obviously too short. My carpenters had never stood back and looked at their work. Half a day wasted.

Stretching my legs and really looking at what I am doing is how I catch dumb blunders. It is true, sometimes you can't see the woods because the trees block the view.

That old carpenter may have been lining up walls with a plumb bob hanging from a tree limb or maybe he was just looking for obvious mistakes.

Seeing the big picture is part of real estate investing too, but only if you keep looking at it. Looking means thinking clearly, not with rose colored glasses. Here are examples of mistakes worth noting.

- Refinancing a year before selling, who is paying those fees?
- Selling simply because you make money, what's the plan for that money?
- Remodeling without a financial payback.
- Failing to consider tax consequences.
- Taking on more than is prudent
- Risking everything when there is another way.
- Flat out dismissing mentor or spousal input
- Add your own mistakes to this list.

Chapter 5

Great Tenants

Chicken war

This house on 60th in Portland's eastside was a little two bedroom with a rickety garage out back. We acquired it in the eighties, within a year the garage fell over. It was a nice place but smaller and cheaper than the surrounding ones. The house fronted on a quiet paved street with sidewalks, a gravel alley ran along one side making it a corner property. The homes main bedroom paralleled the alley with barely a few feet between the window and the dirt track. The neighbor house on the other side of the alley faced another street, so the alley was actually behind their backyard.

The neighbors across the alley were a Russian family with a mob of young blond boys and girls all dressed gaily with sashes and brightly colored shirts.

I knew the kids and spoke with the parents once in awhile when I was in between tenants. They had a half dozen chickens they raised loose in the alley scampering between bicycles, cars and other pets the kids collected.

My tenant was a single guy in his thirties. I knew nothing about him except he worked nights as a mechanic in a 4 x 4 shop. For some reason I drove by the house one day and noticed tarps draped over the front windows. I thought it was odd, but he worked nights, so maybe it was his idea of curtains.

One day he gave notice and moved out saying something about getting married and living with her. The tarps were still covering the windows when I let myself inside, their purpose immediately obvious. The windows were broken, but not just cracked they were shot out. Some of the walls were bullet riddled, used for target practice. Other than that the house wasn't half bad.

When I went outside in the alley to survey the rest of the house the older of the neighbor kids told me my tenant had killed his rooster, shot from the bedroom window at sun up one morning. To say I was shocked is an understatement, what could I say to this boy that has lost his pet.

I apologized, put the house back together, and found a new tenant.

Surprisingly, about six months later, the same gun toting tenant called me asking if I had a vacant rental. Apparently his wedding fell through.

Leasing versus renting

I chuckle a little thinking about this non issue. I know academia trained rental manager gurus out there will quickly chime in listing all the pros and cons. I chuckle because I don't think it matters. As an experienced pragmatist, I know that in every tenant landlord relationship it boils down to trust and doing what you agreed to do and not a piece of paper denoting thirty day or one year agreements.

Let's say a renter is living on the edge with a thirty day tenancy. That's the default when there is no contract or a lease has expired. Now lets say the tenant quits paying the rent. After due process, the landlord tosses out the deadbeat. Now lets say the tenant and landlord have a one year lease with optional extensions in place and the same problem tenant quits paying, same thing, same process, same result, the landlord tosses out the deadbeat.

There are minor differences for sure, but getting your daily rent is not one of them.

Lease versus rent contracts

Having a one year lease or thirty day tenancy or being a squatter makes no difference. The landlord losses his daily rent and must act exactly the same. Throw the bum(s) out.

I have been using descriptive words like deadbeat and bum because it is accurate and reads well, not because I think renters are deadbeats and bums. I hope you see the difference, if you don't, perhaps you need to experience not getting your daily rent, not being able to pay your own obligations, and then come up with your own better description.

Disclaimer aside, lets further analyze rent versus lease. When everyone does what they are supposed to do certain desirable outcomes result.

Lease terms and benefits:
- With a lease the tenant is locked into the contract until a certain date - 12 months - 6 months etc. Landlords like this.
- Rent is set, no increases, tenants like this.
- Everyone has long term stability, this is important for both landlords and tenants. Many times a long relationship develops spanning years. Who wouldn't like that?
- The very fact that you have a lease tends to make things feel more permanent and legal which is a false assumption.
- Some tenants are definitely concerned with maintaining good credit, leases keep them in line. Landlords like tenants that try to be good tenants.

Rent terms and benefits
- Landlords may raise rent with thirty days notice.
- Tenants may vacate with thirty days notice. This is good for tenants not sure of their future. Landlords don't like vacancies.
- Landlords may demand tenant vacate with thirty days notice. Tenants hate this. Some jurisdictions are requiring 60 day notices.

100

The contractual meat of lease and rent agreements is what is important, other than that, rent versus lease is simply short term (thirty days) or long term and what ever you agree to.

Triple net leases

In my never ending quest to do less work and make more money I began using triple net leases or better described as a modified net lease. Triple net is nothing new, most commercial buildings are rented this way Triple net refers to taxes, insurance and maintenance and having the tenant be responsible for them and all ongoing expenses. Plus pay the rent on time.

We still pay the taxes and insurance to make sure it gets paid but pass the cost through to the tenant. The tenant takes care of fixing things including appliances. In theory, I as landlord will get fewer or no calls, except the tenant still needs my occasional approval so I am not off the hook completely. One worry is that the tenant will ignore things because they don't want to pay the bill or do the work. We don't want things like roof leaks ignored.

On the plus side, minor irritants that landlords hate to be bothered with are the tenants problem to solve. A dragging squeaky door, drippy faucet, cleaning gutters or pruning bushes would be good examples.

What I just described (triple net) is not what's normally done, it's what I try to do today. Not all tenants are good candidates for modified lease programs. Some may not be able to do handyman work or refuse to stoop so low to fix something. When I interview rental applicants you can bet I am looking at their ability to pay the rent but their willingness and ability to do minor home tasks is just as important to me.

The rental agreement

The best day in a landlord month is when the new tenant signs the rental agreement and makes payment. Except that's not true, it is simply the last day the new tenant is on their best behavior. The best day is when nothing happens but lets be clear, not getting rent is actually not nothing.

As a practical matter the rental agreement is only a guide of what is expected of both parties. It does not compel anyone to do anything, not even pay the rent. For some of our tenants we end up arguing over a few financial points after or near the end of their tenancy. Chances are the security/cleaning/damage/deposit is in dispute. The last months rent is probably already applied and the move out is completed. The only thing left is disposition of the deposit.

Landlord tenant laws are changing all the time. I think for the protection of tenants primarily. However I have never thought landlords in Oregon are hurting. There are some punitive laws where landlords pay the tenant if certain actions occur such as not giving back the deposit within thirty days or advising in writing any charges. I think for the most part if the landlord treats tenants fairly there will be no dispute. This brings up giving back deposits and what you can charge against deposits and takes us full circle back to the original rental agreement that the landlord prepares.

I have found that I never collect late payment fees. I write it in my rental agreement $25 late fee charge, but I don't insist and let it go. This $25 adds up over the years. The answer is to charge the fees against their deposit but you can't do it unless it states it in the rental agreement. We have a tenant that has been with us for eight years. They are late every single month, I have given them 72 hr notices four or five times. However they always catch up. We have had a number of heated exchanges, honestly I wish they would move out or push me a little too much forcing their eviction. I wonder sometimes if getting my daily rent out of them is worth it.

Here is my $500 worry. I know someday things will end up with them gone, and when they do, provided the unit is still intact, I will have to give them their deposit back even though they have never paid a late fee. The late fee is in our agreement but it does not say that the deposit may be used for that purpose, it is for damage and cleaning. I screwed up by not writing into the rental agreement I will attach their deposit.

Is your compassion showing?

Some hard nosed advisors, authors and bloggers will tell you there is no room for compassion in the landlord business, but you need to understand, that is just their opinion as this book is mine. You run your own show. If you want to let a tenant get behind on the rent, that's fine, that's your decision. If you want to heartlessly evict a family during the Christmas holiday, that's your decision as well.

We have had tenants that were dealt bad hands in life, divorces, deaths, job discrimination. They were trying really hard to support their families. I remember one single father of three that had an ailing mother he was sending money to help support in another state. For several years we helped him. We kept the rent low, we allowed slow pay and no pay. We talked about our struggles as friends do. We never directly talked to him about help, but Linda and I talked to each other and were happy we could make his struggles a little easier. When he moved back east we missed him and wished him well, but we were sure happy to get more rental income from the next tenant.

The two scenarios I outlined were real, you will have your own chances at compassion or hard line decisions. We chose to do both, I only suggest you keep your choices to yourself, your own conscious and not lord over a tenant.

The compassionate Landlord

What we do as landlords can have profound affect on children, I hesitate to say affect on families although it is at times appropriate. Parents are adults and if they acted like adults they wouldn't be getting their kids evicted. Never the less I pay attention to what my actions do to the children. I will never tell a tenant that because of the kids I am being soft, that would just cause the tenant to use the kids as a crutch.

When I contact them if a child answers the door or phone, I do not unload on them saying where is my rent. When I compare my own kids to my tenants kids, I notice a maturity difference. Often times my tenants children are forced into adult roles. Sometimes their parents are barely done being children themselves. We have had lots of grandparent tenants that are in their early thirties. I can't say these kids grow up fast but some are forced into being the adult and I end up having tenant landlord discussions with children. I must say that I have dealt with families run by children that in my opinion are superior to those run by adults.

When I plan serving a notice or setting a court date, I consider Christmas and other holidays. It is very easy to calculate when the family will be moving out. I plan for my own convenience of course but would never boot someone on Easter or at 3pm when school lets out. The kids are not to blame, they are victims.

It seems like now would be a good time to talk compassion. As the landlord there is a very good chance I will know about my tenants family circumstances. I certainly should know who lives in my rental. Sometimes I will know if the parent(s) is playing the system or me or struggling and doing their best. We as landlords can have profound positive and negative effects on others if we choose to. If we think about it, if we act. I am not suggesting being a soft touch, I am merely saying landlording can be more than collecting rent.

Squatters as tenants

A squatter is a person that unlawfully possesses a building or property. That definition would suggest calling the police and having them removed. Except when the police arrive, the squatter says they have permission to be there. So who are the police going to believe? It's not that easy, in most circumstances the police need a court order, a judgement. The police don't settle rental disputes and determine who is telling the truth, even when it is obvious.

In our jurisdiction and I suspect others, the fed court papers allow two names on the defendant line. We always place the primary tenant on one line and the other line insert the words "all others" lawyers will say *et al,* which is Latin for *and others.* A court clerk checking my papers one day made the *all other* suggestion explaining to me that if I evict the tenant by name, the sheriff may only toss out that named person. Another person (squatter) could then claim they have permission and we get nowhere but frustrated. So naming the defendants, *Charlie Tuna and all others* will allow the sheriff to send packing the entire fishy school of squatters.

Who's house is it

Technically it's mine but not mine, and if I have a squatter or someone not paying rent, I still can't come in without their permission. Nor do I want to. However over the years their have been times I entered my rentals uninvited and unannounced. I've done it with trepidation and once or twice outright fear. How come? Well, how about getting shot or assaulted with a baseball bat for starters.

In Oregon we can enter a rental for inspection and some other reasons without permission if we give twenty four hours notice or during some emergency's. I have never done it. I said without permission. If a landlord came into my place when I said no, I would give notice and move, who needs that. That's my feeling, and even though I am a landlord, I am firmly in my tenants corner on this issue.

Now that lines are drawn not to cross I can tell you that after thirty years I have never had an emergency or other reason where I needed to enter a rental against a tenants wishes.

That's not to say I haven't crawled through a window before. I've had tenants go to jail or skip out and believe me, using a window is better than damaging a door by forcing it open.

No cause evictions

I think the smart move is to not say why you want them to move or make up a story such as you are selling the property. Telling a tenant they are to get out against their will never ends on friendly terms.

Our Webster house was in a sketchy neighborhood and we rented to sketchy tenants. Few great people wanted to live there. This one family actually had a mother and father and children but they were street drug dealers including the children. The prior landlord lied to us and I fell for their line of bull. I think the kids drew me in. We became aware of their illegal activities fairly soon after they moved in. Of course the police vice squad knew all about them.

We received a letter from the city vice and drug enforcement division advising us that our tenant was alleged to be involved in illegal activity. The letter went on to explain that the recently enacted city drug house law allowed the city to condemn and board up our property if it turned out that the allegations were true. Arresting and convicting our tenants would be sufficient evidence that we violated the law allowing a drug house to operate. The letter also stated that it was our only warning.

We were in a tough spot, the police wanted us to toss the tenants out of our house and threatened to seize the house if we didn't comply.

I immediately gave them a thirty day notice, serving them in person. I made a potentially fatal mistake when I let it slip that the police were threatening me with the new drug house law and forcing me to make them move out. I was trying to shift blame to the police where it rightfully belonged. The tenant was mad as hell, I got out of there quickly.

When I arrived home in about thirty minutes Linda was really upset, she had just got off the phone with the tenant, he had threatened to kill the police detective that signed the letter. By making that threat I could have served the tenant a 24 hour notice but I wanted no more contact or escalation.

I stayed away from the rental. I planned to file for eviction if they hadn't moved in thirty days. It was a tense time. They moved. The Portland drug house law is unfair and dangerous, it forces landlords to do police work. We never ran afoul again.

Renting to young people

Lots of young people just starting out want to be roommates. I prefer not to rent to roommates unless I have a compelling reason. The problem is that they never last. New couples that are shacking up for the first time are not my first choice either. I like a two year history of staying put.

However our rooming house experiences are not the same as simply renting to young people. I describe our three rooming house rentals and issues in other chapters.

Settling heated disputes.

You would think after reading books and advice blogs about renters and landlords that everyone has an attorney on retainer or needs one pronto. Not only is it not so, it is absurd to think we landlords have that kind of money to throw around. In Oregon we have FED court where landlords go to legally take back possession of their property. The system is simple inexpensive and defendants and plaintiffs routinely represent themselves.

Lets be realistic, if you as a landlord, are careful to screen for normal tenants, you will never need to go to fed court. If you have tenants that don't pay the rent they have to get out, if they don't, you force them, it is as simple as that. The chance that you will use small claims court to collect for extreme damage is next to nothing and if per chance you do, you can represent yourself just like you do in fed court. Attorney representation is allowed, so far I have never needed to use it.

If your head is spinning over my cut and dry comments, you either have a special situation or you are suffering from information overload or fuzzy thinking, possibly both. We have never considered going after a bad tenant for damages or unpaid rent, there is no money in it, none. In our early days we filed in fed court more times than I remember, but we dealt with tenants where that was normal business. I sense clarification is needed for some. FED court is not to collect rent money, although money payments are often negotiated. The FED court is how you get your house back, we as landlords aren't allowed to walk in and take over the property when the rent is late. To legally get possession back in our hands a judge must make a ruling and then the sheriff enforces the courts order. Only after this due process can you take the house back fix it up and rent to someone new.

The bottom line is that landlords should be immensely more inclined to work out a compromise with a tenant. However, if the tenant can't or won't pay the rent that the landlord demands, there is an impasse and time to file papers asap. Why Asap? Because every day waited is a days daily rent not started again, and the daily rent is all we get, the daily rent is what landlording is all about. Of course if the tenant would simply get out when asked, landlording would be easy.

Choosing tenants

In another section I talked about how we follow our gut feeling when choosing tenants. It occurred to me some readers may think, I only rent to people I like. That is wrong, the idea I wanted to get across is that the people I fear or don't like are red flags, so are gut feelings. Trust your gut is not an empty statement, we process information internally non stop every minute of every day, why wouldn't I listen to the results.

Remember, in most cases, prospective tenants are on their best behavior when they meet a property manager that will decide if they get the house or not. In fact we have joked about the stages renters go though, from being perfect people on day one, to calling their landlord names when talking to neighbors, or when disputes arise, to out and out vicious verbal attacks. When they are ex renters it seems the gloves come off and every unhappiness ever experienced becomes the landlords fault.

When a good renter moves out I make a point of offering to provide references and positive reviews. I have noticed that younger tenants and tenants in our nicer better located homes offer reference letters and appreciate positive reference letters or phone calls. I have not had any negative or positive experiences with online reviews. I think it is coming though and some landlords will suffer from phony reviews of themselves and phony reviews posted about prospective tenants.

Sloshing through all the muck of choosing a tenant should not be difficult if landlords simply apply basic rules for each situation. For me and Linda, I don't think we have ever had a split decision. One person or family has always risen to the top. The choice of which applicant or none of the applicants has always been obvious. When we were broke and only one person wanted our house, if they had cash, we grabbed it. At the opposite end of the spectrum, when we have been flush and lots of applicants applied, we have turned them all down and waited until we got what we wanted.

I think a fast formula to follow is to reject first. Throw out all the applications that are deal breakers. Some applicants are so bad in their initial interview it is a wonder they even ask. Next throw out all the ones you personally don't like or fear. Lastly if there are any left choose someone you get along with.

Did I mean fear? Yes exactly. Hope for the best, but plan for the worst. Have you ever heard someone say, *boy I'm glad he or she's on my side, or they have anger issues, or short temper,* I'm sure everyone has. How about the person that unloads on you about life's problems but you know they cause much or their own issues they complain about. Now picture these people no longer your so called friends but with you in their crosshairs as a target of their rage.

These are the people I talk about fearing, I don't enjoy going to battle, verbally or otherwise, so why would I rent to someone that has shown me how good they are at sparring. What happens is that they end up running the show, they dictate to me our landlord tenant relationship. I won't rent to them no matter how good their credit score or reviews are. I'm in charge, I have my gold and I don't share it with people I fear or am uncomfortable being around.

Now let me preface my own fears. If we are hurting financially and need our daily rent, I will make exceptions, If I have only one applicant in two weeks, I can be bought. But I do it with my eyes wide open. I have written about renting to people I know I will be meeting in court in two months. Sometimes one must do what one must to stay afloat.

We don't tell anyone they were rejected or explain why they were not accepted. I tell them I will contact them if they are accepted. I think doing otherwise opens the door to an argument and legal problems. If they call me, I simply say we have accepted someone else or the house is no longer for rent. I may offer to contact them if things change. BUT NO EXPLANATION!

Recently while researching for this book I have had discussions with my grown children and their spouses. All of them are landlord children from birth and some are landlords today in their own right. I expected them to mirror some of my own thoughts and practices. They don't, which reminds me that this book is not an advice book where I tell everyone what to do. It is a book chronicling what we have done including various successes and in my opinion no true failure, setbacks might be close to accurate. My children and my readers may pick and choose anything useful or reject entirely, at their own peril of course.

Abusive renters

Yes, without a doubt renters are rough on houses. That statement is likely to raise the ire of tenants and organizations so I must preface it by saying in my opinion renters are hard on houses. Not just the poor side of town, everywhere. I have commented for years on how I repair damage to rentals that is different than owner occupied. Let's start with break ins. Not only do rentals have a much higher break in rate, but many times the tenants are the culprits. They break into their own homes when they get locked out. We use deadbolts instead of entry key locks to reduce lock outs. Kids damage window screens so often that we quit fixing or replacing them unless the new tenant requests it.

Renters wont think twice about parking on the lawn or digging holes in the yard. They aren't too hot on fertilizer or mowing either. At my home I don't let my kids play on the roof or bounce balls off the walls or the garage door, at rentals it is one big jungle gym playground.

Children are certainly not to blame, lax parenting or lack of parenting allows children to run amok. The same is true of pets, I never blame pets or children for acting like animals, I blame their owners and parents. I think some landlords make a mistake thinking getting a deposit will somehow cause the damage to not happen. That is dumb thinking, where is the financial connection between a dog or a crafty adventurous four year old and a $500 deposit? Is the four year old thinking cash money as he scribbles on textured wall paper, what about the pooch chewing molding or pooping on the lawn everyday? None, the answer is no connection.

The next mistake landlords make with deposits after thinking collecting them cause damage to not happen is to think the deposit will cover the damage when it does happen. That is more dumb thinking. Reality is that the pet probably will cause on going expense. I think that the rent should be adjusted so that all expenses of the house are taken into account. If you offer hot tubs, you have a chlorine expense, bleach damage, large decks, a sealer expense. To make a profit a business must have more income than expenses, it's pretty basic.

If you offer a three bedroom two bathroom house for fair market rent and the prospective tenant asks if pets are okay, of course you will want an additional deposit, but what you really want is additional rent if you expect to cover your costs. $25 monthly is $300 each year that you can spend on grass seed and labor. When I calculate damages and expected rental expenses before they happen, I don't tell the tenant my thought process any more than I tell them how much I paid for the house, that would be asking for an argument. I do negotiate rent when I sense it will seal a deal and sometimes I offer discounts for a few months, but I keep in mind my goal is to pay the bills, including my own and make a profit.

Chopper city

I am sitting on the eight foot wide front steps of my nearly one hundred year old rental. It's a sunny summer day, the big maple in the corner is shading me.   My corner property gives me a view in four directions on two roads. I hear the barely muffled rumble of the engines when they are still five blocks away.   Everyone in the neighborhood hears them.

The chopped and chromed Harley hogs are impressive, so are the burly twenty or thirty something's astride them.   The two

112

swing in barely clearing the sidewalk and back down on the curbs. Their left legs simultaneously shoving out curving kickstands

I was expecting a couple guys, the motorcycles are a bonus. My first inclination is to get rid of them, I don't want a tenant that intimidates or scares me, let alone a matched set. These two with wild long hair, tattoos and arms the size of my shade trees limbs are off to a good start.

"I like this covered porch," says one, "is it okay to barbecue up here?" We walk through the house, each of us asking questions. They are from eastern Oregon, a little town about seven hours drive away.

They said all the right things and had a demeanor that set me at ease. The red flags and my groundless apprehensions evaporated. It wasn't their fault they were big and scary and rode biker gang choppers. Wait a sec. Yes it was. I liked them and ended up renting to them. They were fine tenants, the neighbors loved them and their barbecues. An older longtime neighbor told me they brought stability to the street.

One winter day I stopped by and noticed a chopper in the living room, I was curious how they got it up the steps. It had a cookie sheet drip tray under it, I figured they were on top of things.

They stayed a couple years, I don't remember why they left.

This little landlord story was hardly worth telling, they were so civilized and normal it makes my book boring.

The signal light

Drug dealing is a part of our lives whether we like it or not. You may not see it where you live but it is there. Users make contact and deals go down in restaurants, school bathrooms, taverns, cars, deliveries are dropped off in front of you. In some parts of town neighborhoods are overrun with illicit goings on.

My Beech St duplex was located in the middle of drug central. The building was next to the freeway with an unobstructed view in several directions and an alley alongside. It was a perfect place to watch from or to watch and to escape in a foot race across the freeway or over a pedestrian sky bridge. Police cars could be seen lurking from a few blocks in several directions. When I bought the place it had never occurred to me what a great set up it was for making drug deals. I thought it was two three bedroom units in good shape that would rent for $445 and be suitable for section eight.

The building had an inner porch where transactions could be completed unseen without actually entering the unit. This feature gave the pushers a level of security most of us don't give any thought to.

One morning, I sat in my car parked down the street where I could see the duplex, its porch light glowing like a beacon. I hoped I was able to observe without being seen as a threat. There were early people walking along sidewalks and cars cruising by which I thought odd since it was a dead end street next to the freeway. I watched a car pull up in front, its driver at the wheel while a passenger ran up the six concrete steps and went inside the unlocked door. One minute later the person reappeared. Coming down the steps the person passed one of the sidewalk walkers going up. That person was back out in two minutes. By the time I poured coffee from my thermos the car had made a u-turn and another car pulled up in front nosing into the curb. The driver carrying a bag leapt out taking the steps two at a time. I remember the car, it was an expensive black Mercedes with dark windows and super low profile tires.

I kept my observation post for about an hour. I noticed the foot traffic on the sidewalks increase, people walked back and forth passing by my open window. I saw questioning faces staring at me. More cars pulled in front of my duplex causing small traffic snarls, u-turns became problematic forcing some to back up a full block. I noticed most of the car arrivals were dressed in business casual, some men wore ties, some women in heels. I figured they were all on their way to work. I remember one city taxi cab, the passenger got out while the driver waited. Next a post office mail carrier swung into the curb, its driver, empty handed walked by the mail box and entered the door. He was back in minutes like all the rest.

This procession went on and on, mini vans too, it looked like a convenience store or coffee wagon but then suddenly the sidewalks became empty and the cars quit turning down the street. The show was over, I had to get to going anyway, I was supposed to be fixing something down the street. Before I pulled away, I noticed the porch light was off, it had been daylight for hours, I didn't give it any thought at the time

About a month later, the drug store has moved on and I have a new tenant settled in the duplex. My tenant is a single girl, I think she was drawn to the area due to the low rent and big house. She called after living there for a week, she had a problem and asked for my help. She said that people were coming to her door all hours of the day and night thinking she was someone else, and talking about getting drugs. She asked me who used to live there and if I had any ideas what was going on.

I was embarrassed, I had not told her the recent history, it was my fault she was being bothered. I hedged and fidgeted the conversation for half a minute and then came clean. Ultimately, I told her to turn the porch light off and maybe in a month or two she could try it again. I profusely apologized, I felt bad. Later on, when I spoke with the lady across the street, she complained to me that people were coming to her porch when her light was on.

Apparently, the word on the street was, *it's the place at the end of the street next to the freeway, look for the porch light, if it's on they're open for business.*

Chapter 6

Everyday Landlord

When and where to advertise vacancy's

I have two distinctly contradictory thoughts on this point and not surprisingly I do both. My big picture dictates how I decide.

When I put a sign in the window or out in the yard, I get immediate results. Neighbors often know of people looking for a rental in their area. I don't mean the neighbor next door. Chances are, I already speak with him anyway. I mean the people down the street, around the corner or that their kids know from school.

Prospective tenants that come from word of mouth and signs most likely already know the area. They know the stores, traffic, crime, drug trafficking areas, schools. They don't have surprises that cause them to give notice and get out of Dodge two months after moving in.

New Tenants that come from ads on Craigslist, Trulia or Zillow may have no idea of the local area. They may be shopping price or have bad reviews themselves. If my house is a problem to rent for fair market, I may be better off not renting to a local. If I think the latter I wont put a sign out and will rent it to someone from craigslist.

In almost all cases my prime objective is to get my daily rent flowing again. If possible, I try to find a new tenant while I am getting the house ready. I know that many tenants will have to give thirty days notice and they cannot afford to pay double rent. That means I get stuck in the middle and must lose some daily rent while the clock ticks down.

If I have a remodel opportunity, this is the ideal time to knock it out. I try to have a renter lined up the minute I finish. Not only to get my rent started, but because I know from experience that empty houses get broken into and ransacked. An empty rental is more than lost income, it's a great big target.

> *Why do thieves target empty houses?*

Filing for eviction

Each rental situation is different both in tenant issues and my landlord issues. If I am broke and a tenant is unable to pay the full rent, I might say, how much do you have? I will probably take it with an understanding when I will get the rest. In my neck of the woods (Portland, OR) accepting partial rent means you can not serve them papers and begin eviction proceedings. You must start over next month. In my case, I have all ready considered my options (usually two - evict or not evict) and I have a long term plan (big picture) greatly influenced by short term realities.

If I have already decided to hold the line, it likely means I have reached my limit of patience or I'm broke and I want my property back or I want my rent - no exceptions. By filing court FED papers (forcible entry and detainer they call it, why I don't know) I have made my decision and the clock is ticking. We will go to our first court appearance seven days after I file papers. I will file papers three days after serving the tenant a 72 hour notice. At the first appearance we will set a date for the tenant to move out or we will agree to go to trial in seven more days. With few exceptions there is no defense for not paying rent. The judge will likely grant me immediate restitution of my property giving the tenant twenty four hours to vacate. By going through the process I know with reasonable certainty what day I will get my property back. I can now plan my work schedule. In my case my work is getting the property ready to rent and get my daily cash flow back on line.

I will begin seeking a new tenant right away also. (Landlord secret) We have never gone to trial, appeared in court, yes but in all our fifty plus evictions we have settled without a trial every time. The threat of losing at trial and having to vacate by midnight the next day is much worse than peacefully leaving on a negotiated time schedule. Going to trial is never in my best interest and probably not the tenats either. All I want is a date certain when I get my property back so I go to court planning to make a deal out in the hallway.

119

I will turn down a partial rent offer if I plan to evict. I will serve the tenant a three day notice demanding the full amount. I will do this in a friendly, non threatening, matter of fact, business like manner. I will tell the tenant that if they come up with the full rent, we will throw away the papers, if not, I plan to proceed. I then put it behind me and get on with my day.

When the seventy two hours has expired, I can file at the county courthouse immediately or plan what dates work best for me. Weekends and holidays wreak havoc with expediency.

I know from experience that Mondays are heavy days at FED court so I avoid filing on Mondays, I also know that the sheriffs civil division takes Fridays off and doesn't work weekends so I work that out on the calendar as well. I also know that the court counts complete days starting at midnight so filing or serving papers in the am or pm doesn't matter, your are losing the day no matter what.

These are all little details, but it is surprising how they can add up pushing your eventual reunion with your property out days and then weeks, holding up getting the daily rent started again. Holidays are another pain because they invariably cost you the weekend. Locally, tenants that have been down this road learn a few stalling tactics. One stalling tactic that is particularly annoying is for them to call the court clerk after intentionally missing their first appearance and asking to reset. This little trick is allowed and if the docket is full will buy them seven days. Judges are fully aware of this rule and sometimes show their angst by being not so kind and tossing the tenant out in twenty four hours. Which could easily be sooner than if we negotiated a move out date.

Once we agree on a vacate date, both tenant and landlord must agree in front of the judge, it becomes a judgment. When the date arrives I check the house, if they are not gone, I don't lose my cool, but go to the sheriff's civil service arm and request enforcing the judgement. The next day the sheriff posts the property and after three days at my convenience, the sheriff removes them.

120

To be clear, when the sheriff completes the eviction of a tenant, they come to the house, tell the tenant to get their coat and leave. They do not wait for them to pack or finish eating. If the tenant refuses, the sheriff gets physical and puts them off the property. If the tenant comes back, the local police step in and the tenant is arrested for trespassing. The landlord must store and safeguard the tenants property giving them access to pick it up during reasonable hours.

Sometimes violence erupts and threats are tossed around. When children are involved it is especially uncomfortable. One time I was working for a landlord, my job was to meet the sheriff at 3pm. I did not know the tenant, I was parked out front when the deputies arrived. In a few minutes they escorted the tenant to the sidewalk. Our eyes did not meet while I worked at changing the locks. Then the school bus stopped in front and off jumped three happy children. I watched as the father and his crying kids, barred from entering their old home walked away down the sidewalk. All they had were their coats and school bags.

Over the years in my head I have replayed this image many times, trying to place blame or maybe absolve myself. I never knew any details, I was simply changing locks, but I know I would never let my own children experience what I was part of that day.

> *The eviction process is fairly simple and in most cases does not require legal help. I simply go to the county court where the house is located and ask the clerk for the needed paperwork.*

For me, evictions are sad and emotional, I hate that part of my job. Fortunately it has been more than fifteen years since I evicted someone.

My eviction process

We bought the four plex with squatters living in all four units. The small local bank had repossessed the building and called me, knowing I was game for a challenge. Linda and I inspected the property with the bank executive and his driver, only the driver was really a street tough body guard with a large caliber revolver tucked in his belt.

We made a deal with the bank, I would take the place as is, with squatters and make payments. The interest rate was 9%, my down payment was $1,000 and my willingness to take a big problem off the banks hands.

After inspecting the property but before we left that day I made a short speech to the main group of squatters. There was about a dozen listening,. More were scattered around. I told them they would all be legally evicted in a week and they should look for other places to stay. I was cordial and non threatening, even a little friendly. My intention was to not create waves or give them any reason to vandalize the building. I wanted them to hear the words sheriff and legal eviction. My hope was some of them would fear the system and simply go away.

There is a certain element in our society that is evicted all the time, they know the system and what to expect. Surprisingly this rather sketchy element is sometimes easy to deal with, almost professional.

I filed the required papers, waited the allotted time, went to court and received a default judgment when none of the squatter defendants showed up. Three days later the sheriff arrived for the eviction.

I was parked when the sheriff's civil service officers pulled up. They went inside the building, I sat in my truck, a minute later a group of about six people people carrying bags and backpacks walked out and down the sidewalk. That was it, no fuss, no nothing. This last hold out group knew the system and wasn't leaving until their time was up, then they left without argument.

I heard later that they all moved over to the next block and set up camp again, probably another un fortunate landlord.. As for me I had my hands full. I had four vacancy's and no daily rent coming in, my payments started in a month and all the units needed work and appliances.

FED court is usually held at 9 am Mon - Fri in the county courthouse. The docket may have fifty plus cases and are heard in the order filed. (or so they say) The hallway outside the courtroom is packed with landlords, tenants and attorneys hammering out last minute negotiations.

When each case is called forward the judge asks the defendant (tenant) and landlord (plaintiff) if they have discussed or resolved their dispute. If they answer no, he sends them out in the hall to talk and says come back with a agreement or he will set a trial date in one week.

The hallway starts out packed with experienced landlords leading the fray, thins out when the judge calls cases, and then gets packed again as he sends the newbies out to discuss and settle their differences in the hall.

When I arrive for FED court I find my tenant in the hall and try to have all our negotiations completed and an acceptable agreement before our case is called. When the judge calls us, we tell him our move out date and details, he writes it on the form and it becomes legal.

On a good day, the tenant and I walk out the door together in about two hours. On a bad day the tenant doesn't show, instead calls the court clerk and the clerk reads a message that they are resetting the hearing. I lose my morning and get a parking ticket

Moving day and shrubbery

It would be natural to think I am going to give some pruning tips, well think again. I have long warned people that when they are moving in and moving out, they are prime candidates for getting robbed. It makes sense, it is hard to not look like they are moving.

Landlords get robbed too. When rental houses are turned, everyone knows it and neighbors that covet a rose or flower or bird bath or wind chime or solar light or anything else they can dig up or carry away will do just that. We have confronted neighbors when missing things appear in their yards to hear it was a gift or they bought it from the last tenant. We even had a refrigerator get carted one block away and were told they bought it from my evicted tenant. What can I do - nothing.

Theft

This is a massive problem in the world not just at our rentals, people lie and steal. No consideration is given to right or wrong, rather whether they can get away with it. We have had our appliances stolen, partial cans of landlord white paint, light bulbs, fancy switch plates, floor furnace grates stolen. We had the iron claw feet stolen off an antique bathtub leaving the tub supported by the pipes. The house was listed for sale at the time so many people had access.

When I was doing daily repair work, I warned my helpers and other contractors not to leave their truck unlocked even in front of a job. I told them that if a bad guy thought he could out run him he would grab a tool box and sprint away not even knowing what was in the box. A week later my helper lost his drill that way by leaving his canopy open.

124

One customer rental that I was fixing up, was broken into every single night through an alley side door. Eventually I rebuilt the jambs with angle iron and installed 2 x 4 drop boards. There was nothing to steal but light bulbs, go figure.

My policy was and is, is to never leave tools overnight at a job, building materials can't be avoided sometimes. A new light fixture in a box from Home Depot is a magnet and instant cash for a sneak thief.

Furnace bangs

Early homes had early furnaces and some were known as natural convection systems, some people called them gravity furnaces, but I like the name octopus burners.

Octopus furnaces have a firebox that burns coal or sawdust, or if updated, oil or gas. This one was oil. The furnace sat on a small concrete slab in the basement. The basement had full headroom but the rerst of the floor was dirt. Each room that required heat had a separate duct running to it. Seven rooms seven ducts. Each duct emerged from the furnace at its own port on top. These old systems had no fan, hot air rises naturally, so all the ducts must be run uphill, no dips or level spots, always up. Using natural convection or gravity required large ducts, some were twenty inches. With all these massive ducts twisting and bending their way up and out of the basement, you can see how the name octopus came into being.

My tenant complained that the furnace after heating up made loud popping sounds. The air came out nice and heated the house but the bangs didn't sound right. I investigated when it was cool and reached inside the exhaust where it went into the brick chimney. I brought out pieces of a box of 38 caliber bullets, half of them had exploded. Apparently furnaces are not smart places to hide your ammunition.

Summer comedy

Not all landlord stories are horror tales, some become family treasures. My children grew up helping me and took on projects on their own when they were older. My son was about seventeen and was rebuilding a large front porch that had terminal rot in a post. I paid him of course, I was thrilled to keep the money in the family and help him develop skills.

It was a gorgeous summer day, the house was vacant, a large tree shaded the work area, his jeep was parked at the curb its radio blaring. All in all a pretty nice set up for a carpenter at work.

The porch was about eight feet by twenty five feet with a flight of six or seven steps leading up the middle. There were three large square pillars supporting the roof. Tristan had removed most of the siding and sheathing exposing the inside of one pillar. It was made of short pieces of what looked like scraps, all assembled into a wiggly mish mash of cubes from floor to roof.

Tristan called me at home, he needed help right away. The pillar was bulging and was about to collapse.   He was standing next to it holding it up, if he let go, it will crash and half the roof would fall.

"Are you sure," I said when he called. "Positive," he said, "I can't move, I can't let go, I'm leaning against it holding it up, hurry."

I got there in under thirty minutes, he was stuck unable to move or everything would come crashing down. Just out of his reach were some 2x4's, I quickly nailed up some braces being careful not to laugh at his predicament until after I made it secure.

I didn't stick around, it was his project. Today he manages commercial building jobs. He doesn't call me for help.

As god is my witness

One time at our Beech St place I evicted the tenant for non payment. The eviction went like most, I filed and posted notices, the tenant did not show up for court. I received a default judgment and restitution of my property. I paid the twenty dollar fee and had the sheriff post the property so I knew I was getting possession in three days whether the tenant agreed or not.

The neighborhood was a quiet area of mowed lawns, blooming flowers, no traffic and shaded sidewalks in front of well kept two story houses and plexes.

I parked at the curb in front. The tenant was a very large lady and tall, she did sort of a penguin walk as she made her way up the sidewalk away from me. I think she was walking to her new place for the last time. I don't remember her carrying anything but she was yelling loudly. Her voice was echoing off the two story buildings like a canyon wall answering hello's. It seemed like time was on hold or slowed down. She repeated a chant while she worked her way slowly up the street.

Again and again she said, "As god is my witness, I'm going to get even. As god is my witness, I'm going to get you."

Needless to say, after that when I worked over there I had a hard time not thinking about her parting words and taking worried glances over my shoulder. I never heard of or saw her again.

> *As god is my witness, I'm going to get even*
> *as god is my witness, I'm going to get you.*

When mom's gone

This house is a rather nice middle class four bedroom home in a neighborhood subdivision far from our earlier areas. There is a basketball hoop out in the quiet street. The tenant was a single mom with three kids, two in high school and a middle schooler. I met her and her boyfriend when she applied. The boyfriend lived elsewhere but told me that he was the father figure the kids knew and he would be around for her and them. The mother worked nearby. She drove a dependable old nondescript sedan.

They lived there for less than a year, the kids were in school. I came by to make simple repairs a few times. I noticed how trashy the house was, junk everywhere, the kitchen full of garbage, pizza boxes and dirty dishes.

Then the rent quit arriving. I could not reach her and my door knocks went unanswered. I finally called her boyfriend at his work, he was pissed that I called him and let me know it. I explained he as much as told me to when he said he was the de facto father figure.

The boyfriend cooled some and then told me that the mom had been convicted of a drug crime and was serving a year in jail. The kids were taken away by children's services.

Linda and I safeguarded the family belongings for awhile. We gathered up pictures of her kids cleaned up the house and found a new tenant.

She never came back, never came for her stuff. We still own the house, finding us is very easy if one wanted to. We still have her kids pictures.

We help out when we can, if we can, it's not the kids fault that there parents have issues. When the county or state step in its over.

I really don't care

In another part of the book I recalled a story where a contractor brought the building inspector down on him delaying the project and costing big bucks Here is another bad news bozo that pretty much deserved what he got. I saw it coming minutes after I arrived, I just didn't know what or where.

It was a residential property with scarce on street parking that only got worse at night when all the people with jobs came home looking for a spot near their house. My job was to use my excavator to prep for a short retaining wall along the sidewalk. The owner contractor was flipping the house asap and doing some quick improvements.

When I arrived I noticed he had placed a forty yard trash dumpster in front of the neighbors house, the area at his property was clear. I questioned him saying the next door home owner won't like it. He said he didn't care, it was right on the edge and he needed clear space to get trucks in and out, my excavator included.

Then he said it again, "I really don't care what they say, it's a public street, it's not my problem."

I shut up and did my job, two hours later I loaded up and left. A few months later this same contractor hired me again for a job clear across town. This project was a small apartment complex he was bringing back from near death. The main street had little traffic, around back was an alley that provided access to a full block of backyards on both streets. My job was to meet some gravel trucks and move gravel on to the property.

He said block the alley with the delivery. Of course I questioned the logic of blocking the alley, when we had other choices. I prefer dumping loads in the street if there is room for cars to get by. I never hire flaggers, most drivers are pretty smart and can figure out what to do.

But here is the crux of this recounting.

Again he said, "I don't care."

And then he added with emphasis and an icy stare, "I really don't care." We are talking about blocking the alley, cars won't be able to get by until I clean up the gravel delivery which will take a few hours.

Don't care #2

Shortly, he left and I went to work. While I moved gravel I was thinking how I don't agree at all with his management style, if that's what it's called.

I found out later that the lady he parked the dumpster in front of called the city compliance inspectors. He was cited for removing and placing asbestos siding in the dumpster without permits or following abatement procedures. I think it cost him $12,000. The apartment where I spread gravel was vandalized that night. Connected, I don't know.

When I worked for him, we had been landlords for fifteen years. Back then or today when I work at one of our properties, but especially a new purchase, I look for neighbors watching and eagerly stop and chat. I want to become and stay friends. My renters will come and go, but I'm the owner and the neighbors are my neighbors and will be there to the end.

I offer my neighbors help where I can, If I am making a dump run, I say throw it on. I offer to share, and above all else, I don't park in front of their homes.

I really do care.

The inner cynic

Cynicism is something to be controlled and not allowed to run rampant. Agreed? By definition, cynicism is an inclination to believe that people are motivated purely by self-interest. That doesn't sound too far off. Who wouldn't put themselves first, especially where money is involved.

Synonyms of cynic are, disbeliever, doubter, detractor, pessimist, skeptic. Okay, I see a little of myself. My short story about watching peoples feet rather than what they say is proof of that.

More synonyms of cynicism are, distrust, bitterness, and sarcasm. This is where I draw my line, or do I? I trust people to do what they say, at first. I know I get pissed off when they screw me over, but I don't think I am bitter afterwards, just more skeptical in the future. Sarcastic, yes, I make jokes about situations people get into, I'm not really mocking anyone but I'm not the one to know, am I.

I try to absolve myself of any bad behavior responsibility by thinking I am simply pragmatic and reacting to the truth, facts of life if you may.

A fundamental truth is that people don't appreciate being the butt of jokes or included in a group being disparaged. There is a huge difference between cynicism and bigotry or prejudicial actions but cynicism may be gateway thinking. I think it is virtually impossible to be innocent and pure of thought all the time. The problem is when we open our mouths there is always someone ready and willing to take offense and also someone eager to jump on board.

I truly respect renters, it's all the people that bother me. Oops, was that levity or cynicism or just outdated humor. I try to see other peoples big picture before I go all to pieces shouting road rage obscenities.

I think the inner cynic needs self control in landlording, both for your own sanity and so that you don't pass through the door to bigotry, become an ass, and then make dumb decisions.

It is very true that we rented to a lot of sketchy people. I liked Karen, she was a bubbly enthusiastic single girl with three children that lived in our Webster house. The two story house was the second one from the corner on a quiet barely driven street. It was one block to a busy neighborhood corner grocery. The store was a small jam packed re purposed old house. It had a hot deli case with fried tater's, fried burritos and of course fried chicken. They also sold all the usual staples like 40 oz malts and ice beer, white bread and fortified wine. Also fortified but with steel bars were the windows and door. On the corner outside was a semi permanent assortment of unsavory looking people always waiting for the bus but never getting on when one stopped every fifteen minutes. The police were regulars too, sometimes they just sat in their car blocking the fifteen minute space, but they never caused any trouble.

Karen, my tenant, was about nineteen. I stopped by mid morning to see about the rent. It was a clear brisk fall day the door was ajar, I could hear the baby crying inside. I knocked and knocked making sure she could hear me upstairs, next door and across the street. She never came out. Normally I wouldn't go inside uninvited but my knocking pushed the door open, and the crying concerned me. I strode in on this day. I called her name as I made my way through the front room and to the kitchen. The baby was wailing somewhere, hearing my calls it began sounding more pissed off than in pain. Karen was absent.

The first thing I see in the kitchen is the glowing red elements from the oven, its door open. I feel the radiant heat hit my face from across the room. I place my hand on the cabinets above the stove and to each side feeling the scorched varnish and then turn the knobs off. I call up the stairs one last time and head for the front door. The baby's crying has turned to sobbing, I feel sorry for it.

As I walk by the driveway I check the gas meter on the side of the house. The valve is turned off. The house has a gas furnace but if the

132

bill isn't paid there's no heat. The open oven trick is not new to me, I have replaced burned up elements and re strung melted wires before.

I head for the corner grocery and run into Karen around the corner on the sidewalk. We walk back to the house together.

Once we get inside it is difficult to hold my tongue about the baby being alone but I let her have it over the oven. I went on and on telling her the old house would go up in flames so fast it couldn't be stopped.

I calmed down after awhile, I don't remember where we left the rent issue, I remember we talked for a long time about her plans for the future. She was upbeat and laughed easy. Most young people talk about their dreams to do great things and going back to school or some sort of training. Not her. She said all she wanted to do was gang bang with her gangsta friends. She made it sound like it was something to strive for. I was shocked, a girl, a mother, it made no sense. It was like someone told me of a new career choice for young women. I still don't really grasp it.

I think she may have given notice rather than pay the rent so I applied the last months rent.   Right after she moved out a person called me saying he was going to meet me and walk through the house. He said he wanted to make sure she got her damage deposit back. I agreed and we met at the house, her gangsta friends and gang banging comments still fresh in my memory.

Both of us were on time, he dressed and looked the part , skull cap, tats and sagged pants. The uniform of the streets. He was pleasant enough but I was thankful he was by himself. I brought cash but no extra, my habit had been to empty my wallet sticking extra cash under the car seat, I guess that was prudent but seems prejudicial stereotyping an entire neighborhood and group of people.

We walked quickly through the house, my adrenalin pumping overtime ever since I took the freeway exit. The house was mostly okay, I gave him the cash and he left. I changed the locks and made a to do list. Before I left I taped a for rent sign in the window and pounded another sign in the yard. My heart rate was back down. I pulled my van around to the corner store for a snack, the parking spot was empty, the police car was gone.

When kids strike

Children of tenants can be a real pain, I always take care to listen and talk to them. I have even brought them toys I have come across. Neighborhood children are just as important to befriend, maybe even more important than tenant children. Kids of certain ages with lousy parenting think nothing of heaving rocks through your houses windows or your car for that matter. They will also kick apart fences and porch railings for the fun of it. These are normal kids doing dumb things, imagine if they didn't like you or perceived you had wronged them.

I asked a tenant to move out of my Webster house, I didn't evict them, I gave them thirty days notice. The parents were angry with me and I am sure they voiced their anger every day while they looked for a place to live.

When I got the house back I fixed it up to sell. I overhauled the yard with flowers, shrubbery, sod lawn and bark dust. It looked really good.

The next day when I arrived in the morning the street in front of my property was covered in landscaping debris. Someone had ransacked the yard. Every single plant in that yard had been pulled out and tossed in the street, bark dust and sheets of sod was strewn about. It was a real mess.

I knew that my last tenant had moved a few blocks over. I figured their kids had come by in the dark but I don't doubt that the parents may have done it. It could've been a family outing, I don't know. While I cleaned up the mess and salvaged what bushes I could. I worried that the next night would repeat itself. I considered staying into the evening hours but thought better of it. Escalating things can never work out well. It turned out to be a one time event. I never had any more problems.

Eventually I found a buyer.

I wrote almost two hundred pages of rough draft for this book before I decided to include this story. Originally I was going to exclude it as too horrific or possibly gratuitous on my part. Then I thought about Dave and how he deserved to have the story told and printed.

Our four-plex was a mistake for all of us, I wrote about it elsewhere but left out a major detail that I will correct now.

The building was a converted home, a very big expensive place with a huge front entry, wide steps, and covered, pillared porch. The main door had a lock but it was always propped open or unlocked, inside were four separate apartment doors, two up the grand stairs and two on the main level.

Gang members and general bad guys had taken over the entry and porch, they weren't in the apartments, just the palatial porch and inside stairs. The bottom and largest unit was vacant and I was advertising for a tenant. Not just any tenant, I wanted someone to be my manager. I needed someone to keep an eye on things for the sake of the other three tenants and be responsible.

When I met Dave, we walked the property, he seemed right at home, it was his neighborhood. He was certainly not intimidated, he told me he would make sure things stayed cool. He smacked a stubby baseball bat into the palm of his hand to accentuate his words. Its been a long time, but I still remember him smacking that bat in his hand.

Dave was there for a couple months, he had a girlfriend sharing the place. Then one evening she called me. Dave was dead she said. He was shot in front of the house. Later, witnesses told me he had yelled at a person in a car that had thrown out some chicken bones. The person shot from his car hitting Dave where he stood on the four-plex walkway.

When I got there the next day, there was no police tape, no chalk, nothing at all to tell Dave had lived there. The apartment was open and mostly empty. I hope his girlfriend got his stuff, maybe the neighbors ransacked it. It was as if Dave had never been there.

The newspaper gave him some notoriety, he was listed as Portland's first gang murder. Over the years I have watched for a report of the police finding the suspect. I've seen his name mentioned once, I believe his murder is still unsolved. Dave was happy, and friendly, I think he was in his thirties. His face has faded in my memory but I remember him smacking his palm with the bat saying he would handle things.

Death on my porch

Again I wrestled with including certain episodes in the book. Since I began writing I realized I was painting landlording in a bad light. The truth is, most people will never have the issues we have had, most will have boring investments and make some money. Some will undoubtedly have their own horrors to address. With this book my stated goal is to help others and sell some ink.

Our Webster house is a recurring background for many stories, it was also a background for news broadcasts. Our family joked about it because several times when watching the news a reporter would be standing on the corner sidewalk a block or two from some sort of police action, our house visible in the background. My son or daughter would mention, "hey, I saw your house on TV again." It was always my house, not our house. It's funny how people disassociate with undesirable issues.

The Webster house happened to be on a side street one block away from a notorious corner intersection hot spot of police activity. Of course field reporters set up their interviews and cameras near by but back out of the way.

Now that I have painted the mental picture, I will connect the dots. Gunshots echoed through the neighborhood, presumably a drive by shooting or fight had happened again up on the   **137** corner. People scattered, running away. One wounded man ran to a house looking to escape and seeking help. He struggled to other houses banging on doors. All closed. He ran around the corner and onto the porch of our Webster house where he fell and died.

The next day in the morning, I went to the rental expecting yellow police tape, chalk on the sidewalk, all the stuff you see on TV shows. I parked in front, as usual, the street was empty, no other parked cars or traffic. It was Just like Daves murder at our four-plex one mile away, nothing at all. No police, no people. Nothing to mark the passing of another life. I walked up the four or five steps to the broad covered porch, my tenant wasn't home. A two foot patch of dried blood marked where he fell on the artificial turf I had stapled to the porch. I hosed it down erasing the only evidence that anything had happened. We continued to see our house from time to time as background for reporters news story's.

I included these story's, not because of landlord significance, but because these people were part of our world and deserve to be remembered.

Slumlord or landlord

For what it is worth my opinions may favor viewing my own actions in the best light. Our second house purchased in the eighties was a run down mess. It had not been occupied for five years. The broken out and rotting windows were the old double hung type with wood sashes needing a book or stick to hold them up. The basement storage area had a dirt floor and was only accessed from an outside cellar door. The chimney was crumbling and bricks had fallen inside blocking the furnace flue. All the pipes had frozen and burst.

I fixed everything by myself, this was before I had employees. It took a month or so. When I was done the house looked much the same but was comfortable and was needing nothing. It had heat, weather stripping, secure doors and windows, hot water. It was also nearing one hundred years old and in a bad part of town. Crime was rampant, drugs are on the street and the only person wanting to rent the house is either a bad guy or can't afford anything else.

So am I a slumlord? The house is a shack I admit that. My tenants and their friends break windows and kick in the doors like clockwork. Every other renter ends up being evicted or thrown in jail for drug dealing. The rest disappear. I fix up the house again and again renting it to the next nice person with two months cash rent and a promise to behave.

No I'm not a slumlord and never have been. I used to own some slummy places but I take good care of my tenants. I fix broken things, make sure the heat works and they have functioning locks. I can't fix things out of my control or beyond my yard and I can't erase my tenants checkered past or pick their friends. What I can do is rent to them and treat them fairly.

Famous slumlords in the news usually haven't repaired things like heating and hot water systems. They have drafty leaky houses and refuse to provide basic needs for their tenants.

I really can't say much about slumlords because I don't know any, or work for any. I do hear from my tenants about landlords that have cheated them.

Tenant rip offs

My information comes directly from tenants that have been ripped off. You should not be surprised how many crooked landlords are out there. They teach rental management 101 to a fresh batch of rental managers every semester so the problem will never go away. No they are not teaching how to be bad, bad people take advantage of their positions and resources.

Two primary cons are being perpetrated on innocent tenants. On day number one they are asked to pay a fee to make application. On their last day after they move out, the landlord or manager claims all or more of the deposit than they should. There are any number of swindlers that impersonate landlords and then steal deposits and rent but that is another story all together.

1st rip off. Application fees are   charged by most managers, the ruse is to collect non refundable fees, not rent the unit. Jurisdictions crack down on this but it still goes on.

2nd rip off. Pet deposits are collected with no intention of a refund. At termination, they claim part or all of deposit no matter what. Photo proof at move in may help, but what's that smell? The tenant loses his entire pet deposit.

3rd rip off. Damage deposits are never refunded. The manager inspects and finds inconsequential or nonexistent issues. A single bread crumb in a kitchen drawer will require professional cleaning. A nail hole will require painting. Carpets must be cleaned. It smells. The tenants problem is that they have no argument or power except the court system. The manager was taught to document everything and may do whatever he wants. Including phony photos. They know they
140   are in charge and some take advantage. The repair fees they

charge are never fair. They may not fix anything, pocketing the entire deposit.

Landlords and property managers that take advantage of tenants give us all a black eye. In my opinion it is petty thievery and should be called out.

Chapter 7

Buying & Selling Rentals

The date molded into the corner sidewalk near where we stood read 1912.

I had just finished two weeks of work and was talking with the owner. He owed me around $1,500 for my time and materials, mostly time. Ron had owned the rental house for thirty years after his dad gave it to him.

We agreed that what he owed me for fixing it up and getting it ready for sale would be the down payment and I would make monthly payments at 10% apr and 30 year amortization. The price was $17,500. That's right I had been paid to fix up what soon would become my own rental house. How sweet is that. I think rents back then were about $245 a month and my payments were around $225. Whoopee positive cash flow, then we bought insurance and the furnace needed service. Poof, went my cash flow.

We ended up raising the roof, building a dormer and turning a large two bedroom into a large three bedroom. Of course we upped the rent accordingly.

*Landlord is not the same
as property manager*

*Landlords own their jobs
Property managers may quit theirs*

Location location location

Almost all property has CCR's, covenants, codes, restrictions. Many are ignored or unknown if people skip their homework. They may find they can't park a boat or RV on their property, in the driveway, or in the street. Fences, paint color, roofing, siding, remodeling, all may require approval, nothing is immune from rules.

Most people don't know that subdivisions may have dormant CC&R's that are not enforced or that are yet to be put in place. It's like a secret future headache waiting for someone to step on the wrong toes or raise a few pets that resemble farm animals. Hidden in legal language in the deed is a provision to form hoa's and implement ccr's if someone petitions for a vote.

Potential tenants, just like buyers look for good schools and good neighborhoods. A home with a perceived bad school will not rent for as much and may be harder to find a tenant, of course it will sell for less too.

We owned a home on a dead end street next to the freeway. The traffic noise made it impossible to have a conversation in the yard. During rush hour, traffic slowed to a crawl and the fumes were nauseating. After ODOT built a twenty foot concrete wall the problem went away and the three bedroom rental became sought after.

One house we owned was not hooked up to the sewer system, it had a cess pool, an antique system not used today. When the sewer came through we were obliged to pay for the upgrade, plus hook up within eighteen months. The same property was slated for new sidewalks prior to our purchase. Total cost for sewer and sidewalks was $16,000. We paid $22,000 for the house ten years earlier. The final assessment costs with interest and fees added up to more than the house was worth.

Location and doing research does matter.

Lately, homeless camps have sprouted on hiking trails, and neighborhood paths have long been used as back alleys to nicer neighborhoods. These paths are a thief's dream come true.

We owned a new house in a twenty unit development neighborhood where the builder kept 90% of the homes as rentals. To this day it is a rental neighborhood and lower values are obvious. So is deferred maintenance. Location does matter

50k left on the table

The rental business is full of opportunity to make mistakes. Some mistakes are impossible to spot. Some situations may be red flag warnings to run away from. This story and its outcome boiled down to a gut feeling and a sports car forum.

One of our vacation rentals had been listed for sale for many years. Following my own advice of never selling at a loss I was holding out for my price. A guy answered my craigslist ad and was very excited and wanted to buy not only the one house but both beach houses and our mountain house as well. He would buy our complete turn key vacation rental business.

This was the perfect answer to our wish to retire, one deal, one buyer and we will be on our way to our golden years.

Readers should recognize from other sections of this book that we are expressing our true wants which are to retire and this person is answering our call.

He came to our house and we talked for several hours. In our discussion we moved ahead rapidly. I said we would sell him a beach property on contract but only one and then later sell him another and another after seeing how things worked out. We talked of 35k for a down payment on each house and when I suggested more he was agreeable to go to 50k and make monthly payments.

During our meeting he presented his college achievements and ongoing business affairs, he was very busy with his hands in many things, but never really explained how he made money, he talked about how he was going to make money in the future and was in the process of buying a strip mall and developing warehouses. We concluded the meeting, I said we would consider everything and get back to him.

I went online and searched all I could about him and the company's he owned, sure enough it was all there, even a warehouse in town with a half dozen exotic cars he had for sale. On a whim I searched for car clubs and found his name in a sports car forum. A man in England was warning people that he had paid this person 50k to buy a car and a year later had still not received the car.

We turned away from the deal. It was hard to leave 50K on the table and not get our retirement plan kicked into high gear. I have no idea where our person was headed. I know we could easily get our property back if he didn't make payments but I was very concerned that he was trouble with a capital T. Sorry I have no further info on him, I am as curious as you are.

We walked away from that deal. It doesn't mean we lost out, it means we won. We will never know how bad it could have been. Six months later we did a triple net lease with a local family. No 50k on the table. Just a gut feeling that we feel good about.

> *If it sounds too good to be true,*
> *what do you think?*

Why sell any house?

I guess if you are a flipper, you sell to make money. I am a landlord, I collect rent to make money. I am also a real estate investor, as such I realize that the instant I sell my property I am no longer invested. In the stock market when a person sells his blue chip stock just before the price soars, he regrets not being invested anymore, he quit, he sold out. As a real estate investor, I know I must stay an owner to be invested. Stocks pay dividends and go up in value. Property earns rent and goes up. Same thing in my mind.

So to answer the question of , "why sell," for me, I sell when I want the cash to buy something. For example when we built our home where we live today, we needed money to pave the driveway, buy cabinets and install hardwood floors. I also wanted a tractor and a bigger sailboat. We cashed in a duplex, set aside the capital gain tax money and moved ahead finishing our house.

Another reason to sell, was to improve or expand our business. If we came across a deal that excited us, we would sell something we didn't like and do a 1031 exchange. As I think back, we have several chain exchanges where we have done multiple buys and sells spanning decades, always deferring the tax burden. Our Mt Hood cabin has two 1031's leading up to its purchase. Another paid off home has three exchanges in its history with us.

Why sell? It's the only way to quit your job. You are essentially selling your company in order to resign your job, a dilemma we face today. It used to be that you could earn 10% or more on a bank cd or certain accounts, so putting cash in the bank was once my plan to retire, not anymore. It has been a long time since banks paid a worthwhile return, I'm not expecting a change in the near future. Consequentially we are not willing to sell off our only income with no replacement in sight.

Selling property at a profit or that we depreciated for many years incurs an income tax. Selling property that we did a 1031 exchange has a deferred gain that must be paid. As a rule of thumb I anticipate losing 33% of our sale price to taxes when we sell property. Maybe that is one reason we have stayed landlords for so long. That same 1/3 of our property is making us money each month and I don't want to give it up.

Today we are selling some property on private contracts, and triple net lease options. We still have to pay taxes but it is spread out over long periods minimizing the pain.

In a sense we are trading collecting rent for collecting interest. We are trading management responsibilities for potential appreciation. We still have little cash to throw around but our real estate is supporting us and I don't see us outliving the contracts. Our children will be pleased someday. Maybe.

> Buying rentals is buying a job
> A job you can't quit

There is a real argument for both scenarios. We currently live about two miles from our nearest rental and two hours (90 miles) from our furthest home.

Okay I fibbed, The arguments are not equal or even close. Having a rental two hours away means that in any given day I will spend four hours driving and with eight hours of work end up with a very tiring twelve hour day. Doing this stunt day after day for a major fix up or remodel is horrible. Driving by your self is even worse. It means that work gets put off or you must hire someone.

Property that is fifteen or twenty minutes drive is just about perfect. If a water heater needs an element, a door needs adjusting or you want to meet a contractor to go over a bid, you can head for the rental after lunch and be home early. Better than bankers hours.

I find it extremely difficult to bring with me every possible tool I may need for routine repairs so being able to run home is invaluable. I have quite a few extra hacksaws, screwdrivers and wrenches and much more I have purchased at the local Ace store because I did not have one with me two hours from home. One time I bought a three inch slip joint pliers for a toilet tank nut ($24.95) otherwise I would have to make a second four hour drive the next day. Similar problems crop up finding a shovel or dab of caulk or paint or even a trouble light.

I would not want a rental in my own neighborhood or my children's school area. Driving by your nearby rental may save you in an emergency but more often it will simply alert you to an irritant. Do you really benefit knowing your tenant parked his car on the lawn, has full time visitors, a huge wolf/dog or believe me, much worse. Not me. I can create enough stress without asking for it with drive by's.

When I find myself near one of my rentals I do not detour even one block for a drive by. In some things, ignorance really is bliss.

Oil tank witch hunts

Run away, as fast and as far as you can. You don't have to buy a headache. Some of our environmental rules bite really hard. I guess it really depends on whether it is you getting bit.

Once upon a time we would yank empty old oil tanks out of the ground, smash and crush them flat and haul them to the landfill. Times have changed.

Typically your realtor will recommend an oil tank search and soil contamination inspection. If you are the buyer that's a good thing, it could be really costly for the seller. It could also nix the sale, costing both of you.

Sam's house, my first rental had a great looking and running oil furnace. It ran flawlessly the entire time I owned the home. There was a 600 hundred gallon tank buried in the yard right next to the concrete basement wall. An oil delivery truck filled the tank once a year, possibly spilling a few drops of oil in the process. No one knows.

When I found a buyer and they requested an inspection it hit me like a gut punch. I knew instantly I was going to the cleaners to be hosed. I had already been involved as an excavation contractor in oil tank removals many times. I knew what was coming.

If a leak is found or contaminated soil is discovered, the EPA must be notified, that's the rule. Repairs or decommissioning are required and the contaminated soil carted away. The laws may be different in your area but I will bet that whatever the law is, it will cost a bundle to become compliant once a problem becomes known.

I reasoned with the buyer to no avail, after all why should they accept responsibility for a system when they don't have to. For me, why should I look for costly trouble with a system that appears to be perfect. A true Pandora's Box if opened. The buyer opened the box, the inspection outfit drilled holes in the yard around the tank and found traces of oil. They reported me to the EPA as required. Now what? The realtor that started everything and their buyer can hit the road leaving me stuck.

As owner of the property, I hold the tainted gold. I can refuse to go ahead with the sale. I can agree to pay the bill and proceed. Now that the box is open and the government is involved I have to do something. Even if I refuse the sale I still have to deal with the EPA, I'm caught like a deer in the government headlights. No matter which way I feint, I will still get hit.

The rest of the story is that I had plans for the money I would receive from the sale. I wanted to quickly move ahead. We closed the deal, setting in escrow a big chunk of change. The tank was decommissioned by a company approved for that work. They pumped it dry and filled it with a concrete slurry. An hvac company installed a brand new gas furnace. All in all it came to about $14,000 to fix a system in a rental that I thought worked perfect.

I have thought about this sequence of events over the years wondering what I could have done differently. I bought Sam's house on a private contract before oil tanks were routinely suspected. The leak, if there even was one, could have started during my tenure. I could have canceled the sale and raised the price to compensate but as I said I wanted the money asap.

I believe that trying to squeeze every last nickel out of a deal, while commendable, is not always the best way to proceed. Keeping the big picture in mind, If there is enough money to get the new project done moving ahead is best. Goals are achieved by making progress, not by canceling sales.

The reality for Sam's house was that I made my profit when I shook Sam's hand and locked in the deal many years earlier. The exact amount does not matter but it enabled me to make many more deals. The final profit from Sam's house may never be fully known.

Buying property with an oil tank and other issues may be a big and costly unknown but you can find out some of the expenses ahead of time if you are so inclined. There is a lot of money to be made in real estate and if you figure into your budget the costs of oil exploration, sewer construction, sidewalk, infrastructure and structural improvements you can succeed. That is not my business. I try to leave that for others. I am a landlord and real estate investor with remodeling skills, not a speculative developer with deep pockets.

Run away as fast as you can
if it smells like oil

1031 exchanges

This program called so from the section 1031 of the internal revenue code is an absolute must for investors like me that have little income to play with. Doing an exchange is like turbo charged compound interest on your equity, it's like borrowing money to invest and never having to pay interest for it.

While it is not too good to be true, the program is not a scheme to get out of paying taxes. I will explain my use of 1031's but remember, do your own homework, I'm not your expert tax advisor.

In a nutshell, when I sold a house, I elected to do a 1031 exchange. I told the closing agent my plans and the name of the 1031 company (facilitator) I chose to use. When the final payout check from the sale was prepared, instead of giving it to me, they gave it to the 1031 company for holding. When I find a new property to buy (exchange), the 1031 company will hand over the money to the new title company, minus their profit and expenses of course. It is not cheap but if a lot of money is involved it pays off big time. The point is, I'm not allowed to handle the money, a 3rd party facilitator holds it, and then pays for the new property. This way they can call it an exchange.

This all happens fast and is really quite simple. Your escrow agent will explain it in English.   If my new property is more money than what I sold I will need to get a loan or kick in more cash for the difference. If my new property is less money, I will have some change coming and possibly a tax bill.

The tax angle savings is this. When you make a profit from the sale of property, the government takes a cut of the profit. That change I had coming is profit and is taxable, some of the money spent to make the new purchase is also profit but is tax deferred in a 1031 exchange. When or if I sell the new property and take the profit, I will then pay the deferred tax and any new tax, or let it ride and do another 1031 exchange.

You make money by letting your profit stay invested and deferring the tax. You may buy and sell many times, always doing 1031's. In essence the money buying your rental is tax money that someday you will have to pay to uncle Sam, but in the meantime the money is free for you to use and collect rent with. There is no time limit or amount limit. You can collect rent until you die using tax deferred money to purchase rentals.

> *It's as close to free money*
> *as you can get*

The dilemma is that we don't want to wait to die just to beat some tax bill. Someday you too will want to cash in your real estate investments and have to pay your long deferred baggage. This is okay so long as you understand that the money is not yours, it is taxes you deferred but still owe. A real cash problem happens when a poor decision maker refinances their rentals and then spends the proceeds. They just spent the tax money they owe. When they sell the house there wont be enough to cover the shortage and they will be in real trouble.

1031 exchanges have a bunch of rules you must follow. You only have forty five days to find a replacement after you sell is one rule. Another is that you must elect to do an exchange when you close the sale, not after you find a replacement. I try to line up my new property before I sell the old one. Twice I have not had a replacement property ready and was rushed into buying places within the time limit. One of the properties was a condo I wish I had passed on. If you change your mind or don't complete the exchange after beginning the process you still have to pay the facilitator fees and of course all the taxes.

If you find a replacement exchange that is more money, you simply kick in the difference like I said, if it is less money you will get a taxable check back. The amount of profit that you receive or keep out of the exchange money is taxable. Profit is taxed, right. Defer taking profit, defer paying the tax.

Again, you don't have to exchange all the profit from the sale. For example, lets say I sell my rental and make a profit of one hundred grand, I can keep all of it and pay the tax, or I can buy a replacement using seventy five from my exchange and keep the other twenty five, of course the twenty five is taxable, the seventy five is tax deferred until I sell, if ever.

To sum this up, it is very easy to create a decent rental income using tax deferred money, it is like borrowing money for investing that has no interest to pay. Free money to purchase rentals is a very good deal for the *Everyday Landlord.*

1031 exchanges are a must for the landlord that understands free leverage

Turning the house fast

This is not a fix it book, but lets talk about fixing things anyway. When I started remodeling projects in my first home in my early twenties I had little knowledge. What I had was confidence that I could figure out how to do things. I look back and remember all the dumb Ideas and poor design choices I made. Confidence does not make you smart, but it gets you going and that is what is important.

If your rental is in a rough part of town, you will have rough tenants and the house will likely be old. Fixing old rough houses requires appropriate thinking not emotional daydreaming. We have never had paychecks to fall back on to carry our rentals during down times, they must support themselves. I think having your *back against the wall* forces one to get the job done. That job is to get the rent flowing asap with minimal expense.

Typically when we got a house back in the bad part of town, it was full of discarded junk. The tenant had no expectation to get their deposit back, we started by making a dump run. Next I make the house secure. During the fix up days, I have no choice but to leave construction materials in the house when I am not there. It is not practical even possible to load up everything at quitting time each day. I load up my tools, I'm not stupid. Boxed goodies like light fixtures or anything that can be carried off are subject to theft.

Most windows must be made functional especially bedroom for legal egress. Broken glass is common, if only a small crack a bead of silicone will suffice and pass a section 8 inspection. Missing glass must be replaced, plywood is okay during fix up only. Latches must be functional.

Entry doors, front and back must be made secure on day one, all other sources of entry into the home and garage or outbuildings must be secured asap.

What's with the locking up obsession. I have plenty of break ins and thefts to support my thinking. A door standing open or window ajar is a invitation to anyone to climb in and see what is laying around.

Turning fast #2

Thieves are among us, I accept it, but not all crooks are the same. A nice lady will walk in an open door, saying "hello, anyone here, is this place for rent," and lift your cell phone off the counter but she wouldn't consider opening a closed front door. A neighbor kid will try the knob on a unlocked closed door and then help himself to your rechargeable drill but he would never kick in the door. He would also lean the garbage can against the wall and slither through an open window but would never use a pry bar on the latch.

More brazen criminals think nothing of shouldering a door open if they see something through a window they can sell or return for store credit. Every bad guy in your neighborhood knows your house, they watch you deliver materials and tools coming in and out. They know they can climb in the back window and the neighbor can't see or won't tell. Your rental is their cash ticket and they live there 24 hours a day. You don't.

The best I can do is minimize my exposure. Bring in the trash can and only use chain link fences. Leave lights on, install motion detector yard lights where they can't be vandalized. Hide from view everything. We have had half cans of paint and light bulbs stolen, nothing is safe and loosing the last of the custom colored paint is a real inconvenience, believe me.

Hiding a key is like handing it to the kid next door. I install combination lock boxes if I need to allow others access regularly.

Condemned houses - why

When we were looking at ODVA property, we bought a five bedroom house. The listing papers showed it had gone no bid several times in spite of being listed very cheap and looking acceptable on a drive by. Maybe it was all the bright orange placards stating the property was condemned.

Our first inclination was to pass, I think that was why it was not sold. I looked into the reason for the condemned designation and found that there had been a small furnace chimney fire requiring a fire department response. The fire chief reported to the building compliance inspector that he thought there was un-permitted remodeling work in the basement. The building inspector then condemned the house. The owner was in trouble financially and lost the house to foreclosure.

Before making my offer I asked the city what was needed to bring the house into compliance and was told I needed to purchase a building permit for the new work.

We bought the house and went down to the permit desk. The building permit cost under $25 and we didn't have to do any work or make any changes.

The lessons learned are several. First, it is important to find out things, not just walk away. Second, I think you can safely assume the city and county departments share information. Since this episode, I have been involved with multiple departments for one reason or another, I know they talk to each other. They also talk with the courts, the police and the utilities. It is not unusual for an inspector or other official to once have worked as a contractor in the field they inspect. It really is a good old boy system.

Not permitted remodeling

Oh boy - what a tangled web we weave - said someone not Shakespeare. Am I about to out myself? I hope not. I don't **157** suggest that anyone not follow the applicable laws. This section is about buying and selling, lets talk.

If you buy a place as is with unpermitted work you may end up being responsible and paying someday. The other side is you may not or it may not cost much. You might negotiate a huge discount over the issue.

You might do a huge remodel, get permits and cover all the unpermitted stuff in the process. So that huge discount was really smart.

You might buy a place and add some bedrooms in the basement and attic, maybe a bathroom or two and raise the rent and never sell, so having a permit is mute.

The permit police will correctly say that inspections are important to make sure things are done correctly. I second that. I have seen atrocious work that is beyond stupid, even dangerous. I have also seen lots of so so work that I would give a pass to.

My policy has been to always think safety first. A sloppy roof flashing that leaks does not rise to the level of a deal breaker, a poorly built railing thirty feet above a moat full of gators needs immediate attention. I would never create a bedroom without legal ingress and egress. I would never plumb a fixture without proper venting or wire a circuit without breakers. The same with collapsing gator railings.

The problems I come across when looking for property have been when I spot old remodeling work that is substandard and not permitted. Sometimes rectifying (fixing) things are more costly than the owner realizes so we are unable to agree on a fair price. I pass. I recommend that readers of this book get a friend that knows real estate and construction to advise them. I am not in favor of so called professional inspections, they are no guarantee that things (very important things) are uncovered. You need a friend. The pros do have nice looking letterheads and fancy check list forms, I will give them that but they don't work for you or have your interests, get a friend you can

158 talk to about your concerns and your big picture.

Pro inspections are part of every transaction today, but their purpose has morphed into a way to weasel lower prices. I believe in using every tool in my bag to get a great deal when I buy, so should everyone. For every buyer there is a seller on the other side. But don't for a second think that a pro inspection is some sort of magic pill for buying property any more than a tenant screening clears the way to getting your daily rent.

In the late eighties we bought a fixer. The price is irrelevant, we paid $500 down payment and 9% apr. The house had been uninhabited for five years. The chimney was collapsing, the water pipes had frozen and burst in over twenty places, carpets, vinyl, formica were all shot. The front and rear porches were unsafe to walk across and most windows were gone. We saw huge potential and bought it as is.

We fixed everything and rented it with positive cash flow for seven years. We sold it for twelve times what we bought it for.

To sum up my thoughts, yes, in our expansion days we would buy a fixer or condemned or unpermitted house in a heartbeat, if the deal was right and the issues were within our means. We made a triple play on that house. We made money remodeling (I paid myself), we made daily rent, we sold out at a great profit and put that profit to use in a 1031 exchange.

Rental hopping

Our children are buying and moving into homes they plan to keep as rentals. They are making improvements for themselves and to maximize rent and then moving on. I must point out that what they are doing is smart leverage of cash and financing but has one draw back. Sooner or later they will outgrow moving from rental to rental and want to stay put.

What makes a good rental is not what makes a great family home. A good rental brings a return commensurate to its value but a family home may have expensive features that don't increase rent. For instance, large lots or acreage, pools, hot tubs, orchards, bonus rooms, out buildings are all desirable for growing family's but do not necessarily increase the rent much.

Flipping versus renting

Except on television, I never hear about people making a living flipping homes. In our little world we talk with our social group which includes other school parents, Boy Scout and Girl Scout parents, teachers, soccer families and a few sailors. It is true, some have told us stories about making a killing in real estate but no one we know flips for a living.

We have sold our share of property and made a profit on every one but I think not collecting rent every month would be scary enough to make me get a job.

For a flipper to make money, they need a rising market or create added value by updating and remodeling. If they are depending on a rising market they are simply pocketing appreciation, what will they do when things level out or the bubble pops again. If they are remodeling to create value then they are earning every penny and putting in hard days. When they stop remodeling so does their income.

For us landlording was a natural extension of my construction work. Sam's house was our first rental, I would never have become aware it was available if not for my doing handyman work. Our next rental, once again was a home I worked on.

My children are grown now but were all born and grew up with landlording. So far, six of seven of them are buying rentals or planning on buying rentals but none of them say they are quitting their day jobs. None of them have flipped any either. I have never overtly pushed landlording on them. We talk some about their remodeling plans and have an active family tool loaning program but they have their own goals and plans. I can't imagine they don't have a few of their own strong opinions regarding real estate and managing rentals, where they got them is a mystery to me.

Trust and lucky deals

Put your money where your mouth is. I believe that finance company's require 20% down payments because they don't trust anyone. They don't trust us to do what we say we will do. They don't trust us to make the payments, pay the taxes or keep the property insured so they make you and I pay into a reserve account.

> *Trust is when you stand under a dead tree on a windy day.*
> *Luck is when you move the car before the tree falls.*

I suppose they have these hard nosed policy's because people dump on them. They also require property to pass an appraisal so if they have to sell it, they wont lose money. Everything makes perfect sense and if you understand why, you are in a good position to make contract offers that get accepted. Offers for private contracts may include anything you can dream up, but acceptance comes down to trust. Trust in you.

I think about contracts and what works for me. I am both seller and buyer on a number of deals so I look at both viewpoints. The seller wants primarily two things. He wants to earn interest income long term, and he doesn't want to be bothered with managing the property anymore.

If you are trustworthy, do what you say, don't make excuses in lieu of performance, and get the job done, you will make all the great deals you want. There are lots of property owners looking for monthly interest income.   Down payments are completely negotiable or not even required. This is where thinking outside the box pays off.

If you can convince the seller that he will get his interest and you will do what ever you have agreed to do, you will make the deal. In fact you will get so many deals coming at you, you will be able to pick and choose. However, deals and luck favor the prepared that are out there looking, not the big talkers who's feet are planted growing roots.

So it is not trust and luck, it is trust and performance, luck has nothing to do with it. Luck is when the tree falls and misses your car. Performance is when you spot the leaning tree and move the car.

Exit Strategy

I have struggled with how to get out of the landlord business for over twenty years. When we were young the banks paid a decent return and I thought I would make my first million, put it in a bank and get $50,000 a year income. Things have changed, what I read and hear now is that we need to have our life's savings in the stock market. Is that the same market that tanked in 2009 and then took ten years rebounding. I think so, or rather, no thanks.

Once upon a time I was on a landscaping job and my customer was an executive at a financial brokerage. His home and property and the way he conducted himself exuded money, plus he was paying me a healthy premium for my tractor work. I thought he might have some valuable mentoring advice. At the time we owned a dozen rentals so naturally conversation drifted to capital gains taxes. He said, "just pay your freight and move on." Easy for him, he had a big income.

He had no answer I wanted to hear, no magic bullet, I figured he should know some secret. He was right though, you should plan to pay your taxes and if you don't squander the money you have set aside, paying your freight should be no problem or surprise.

I have two primary issues with getting out of the landlord business. The first is that I want to shift my work from rental management to something like sitting and doing nothing while earning 10% return. The second bigger problem is that if I cash out (sell my property) I will lose to taxes about a third of my asset base that is currently making me money. In other words a million dollars in income producing rentals becomes six hundred fifty thousand in cash earning 1-2% in a bank or a scary mutual fund ride that might lose my principal. All my 1031 exchanges and depreciation deductions will become due and payable as each property is sold.

My strategy is mine alone and I am not suggesting anyone follow it. I want to share what we are doing, but you must decide what is right for you. I will keep saying, don't do lazy thinking.

We first employed this idea to sell a house that would not pass an appraisal inspection for conventional financing. We had a thirty year mortgage left over from the no-doc days of the ninety's and of course virtually all mortgages have a due on sale clause effectively barring me from a contract sale.

I came up with a lease option with a declining option price. The lease is triple net, where all maintenance, insurance, taxes are the tenants responsibility and added to the monthly bill. The tenant pays everything. With each rent payment made the option purchase price is reduced by an amount equal to what a conventional mortgage payment would reduce principal. In other words, after thirty years the purchase option price is something around $100

I don't believe we are violating the due on sale clause because the property is not sold, it is leased and renewed each year. The tenant is under no obligation to exercise the option. He may walk away at anytime. Obviously as the years pile up so does the discounted price and walking away becomes increasingly foolish.

I also included a fifteen year flipping penalty where the price is increased if they exercise the purchase option early. Fifteen percent the first year reducing to one percent in year fifteen.

I ran this by our cpa and she suggested that the tenant purchasing for a buck will have zero basis and then a big capital gain when they ultimately sell. We of course will have to recapture our fully depreciated basis which will become due the year the option is exercised. Also, all of our income will be taxed for thirty years as ordinary income, where as in a sale the income would have been at a lower capital gain rate, but in one big chunk. These are all baggage details, but none are deal breakers for us.

One aspect I have not been able to get my brain wrapped around is that my children will undoubtedly inherit from me some of these lease options. I hope I am not setting them up for a costly headache.

I have done several declining lease options and plan to do more. We will not create large piles of cash this way but we are accomplishing our goal of reducing day to day management while keeping a monthly income.

While we are talking exit strategy's, there is one method we have not taken advantage of. I think if a person planned wisely they could easily convert through 1031 exchanges rental homes to their personal residence. We have not done this because we built our family home early in our struggles and want to stay in it.

But lets say we did exchange all our property for a private island and then moved there. In theory we would not have to pay the deferred tax but we would have no income or cash either.

Our exit strategy does not exist, I am hopeful something develops.

Chapter 8

Day to day chores

Everyday choices

I can't do everything I want at once. Don't we all wish we could snap our fingers and things magically appear or get done. It does not work that way. In fact Murphy is around every corner waiting to throw a wrench into the best plans. I do know that things tend to go smoother for me than some others I hear about. I attribute good planning and experience to my less than stellar track record. I am my worst enemy at times.

Here are some big picture examples that influence my choices.

- I tend to want to take the money, it's my nature. I would think everyone would. I must balance repairs, showings, evictions with family schedules.
- I get tired of certain people and want them out of my life.
- Certain people, I try to help. (usually my daily rent suffers, but not always)

- I know the house or neighborhood is a disaster, so I am unwilling to put out money or effort for what seems like a lost cause. This is a bad landlord attitude and does not help anything except the landlords bottom line, and even that is arguable.   The name slumlord surfaces nearby.

- A jerk neighbor calls and complains, or worse, files complaints.
This issue really bothers us, we don't like nasty phone calls or nuisance letters from the city.

- My other job is taking all my time.

- I have a long term plan that needs progress made.

- I choose to go sailing on nice days.

So the big picture influences little decisions, ultimately trade offs are made. That is why I have let a bad tenant move in, knowing full well I will be going to court in two months. It also explains why I will let a tenant paint and clean in exchange for part of the deposit, knowing he may screw up both seemingly easy tasks.

Screening tenants

Again, I must warn you, I am not giving advice, I am simply telling my landlord story. We have never paid a tenant screening service, partly because we go back to before the Internet and services became common. In our early years we would put a for rent sign on the corner, or let neighbors and drive by traffic spread the word.

I said before that some managers charge a fee to every applicant, and then rent to none of them, keeping the fees. I suspect the practice is illegal, if not it should be. We have never charged an application fee, in fact we quit using applications. If I am interested in a applicant, I ask them to supply me references, employment verification and their current landlord. A scrap of paper will do, but I prefer an e-mail. I am reluctant to rent to someone that has been in their current home less than two years. I don't want to become the next short timer landlord.

I talk with the tenant quite a bit, share stories, I don't want to be their new best friend, or adopt them. I want them to let their guard down, be themselves. I size them up you might say. I try to visualize what they will be like in a disagreement. Will I fear them after giving them the keys. I don't need to fear my tenants. I want them to behave better than some children I have seen.

I have learned to look for action in people, I tend to dismiss big talk. I also look for liars, good liars can slip by, bad liars I wont rent to. I believe that a liar thinks they can lie about when they will pay the rent and somehow in their head that makes it okay. Sorry Charlie, please accept this 72 hour notice, if you really do pay your rent as you say, you can throw it away.

I also find it very difficult to rent to someone I get a negative gut feeling from or don't get along well with, why should I set myself up to deal with someone that sets off red flags.

One last little repeated point, I never ever tell someone why I wont rent to them, that's an open door for an ugly argument. If I respond at all, I say I haven't decided yet or I have found a tenant.

.

Calling past landlords

Sometimes when I call a landlord they wont talk or they say send a written request, both are red flags for me. I'm just doing my job, I don't want any assignments. I can rent to the next person.

When I talk with a landlord, I don't ask if the tenant was a good or bad tenant. I try to get them to volunteer information and talk. At some point I will ask them if they would rent to them again, if I get a silent pause, I say, "just yes or no, no need to explain." If I wait they will come around and unload all their past tenant troubles and explain anyway.

Recently I asked a landlord if they would rent to the tenant again and he said no, I remained silent and he began telling me his peeves. I decided to rent to the tenant anyway, in spite of the ex landlords issues. Hope I'm right.

I have had current landlords lie to me, tell me the tenant is great, and pays the rent on time. The truth is they are willing to say anything to get the tenant to move away.

Should tenants make repairs

Absolutely not. So why let them do it? Simple, it moves ahead the process of getting the unit back on line. Here's a little obvious secret. Everyone finds fault with someone else's work, but they think their own work is acceptable. Therefore a picky tenant is not likely to complain about their own work.

The downside is that I have never, not even once, had a tenant paint job that was as good as I could do. Same with repairs - cleaning, maybe. When I hire contractors or helpers, I get mixed results. There is a massive difference in skill levels, and fixing up rentals is not the same as remodeling or new construction. With rentals the paint will be repainted repeatedly, today's crappy job may be improved by tomorrows better job. Same with porch, deck, window, floor, counter jobs. It is never ending. In the construction world repair jobs are considered acceptable when completed workmanlike and to normal standards. This is a low bar for any competent craftsman. In the rental business, the bar is much lower. Not lower because workers are not good enough, but lower because it is not cost effective to demand and pay for perfection each time a rental turns.

As we sold and bought rentals, we improved our lot. We bought in better areas, and acquired nicer homes. Consequentially our repair and painting quality had to improve or our business asset suffered in value and rent.

It is common to paint and have a rental ready to go and then have a prospective tenant ask if they can paint it because they want a different color. Years ago I said yes, why not. Today I am not so agreeable. Today I will use a stalling tactic. Let's talk about it in six months.

Tenant move in costs

In thirty years I have not seen much change, people live pay check to pay check. Few of our new tenants can afford to pay double rent during their transition between homes. As the quality of our homes improved so did our tenants. Years ago none of them worried about giving notice, today all of them have to give thirty days notice, and I wholeheartedly agree, after all, I'm the next landlord.

The current landlord still has the deposit and the last months rent. My goal as always is to get the daily rent flowing again. Sometimes it behooves me to let the tenant pay off the deposit and last month rent in payments. Over one to three months is acceptable, six months is not. I also will offer a discounted move in rent if needed. For example I will lower the rent $50 or more for six months and then it goes up to what I want.

These little inducements are particularly helpful with hard to rent or high rent units.

A downside is that if the tenant can't really afford my place, all I'm accomplishing is enabling the tenant to get in over their head, and guess who suffers in the end, that's right everyone.

A very real issue with accepting payments to help with move in costs is that if things go south right away, I have very little of the tenants money and they have my property. They could bail on me or I may have to evict them, in which case I will regret my decisions. The solution is to be very sure of your tenant, helping a good person or family is much better than being hoodwinked by a deadbeat.

Forms forms and lists

While I was thinking about writing this book I looked at the books others have put out. At first I was taken back because just about every book that comes up on an internet search is packed with legal forms or financial charts or both. The authors invariably are attorney firms and management outfits selling their program. I read reviews where customers are exclaiming how handy the forms are and so easy to download. Forms to inventory a rentals condition, check lists for references, job lists and credit scores. People are easily impressed by glitz but it is not the form that the landlords need, it is the information entered on the form. A scrap of paper with a hastily written note is more useful than a blank form.

We use forms, but not the ones they sell or download. I question the usefulness of what I found available. From memory I will list off some. Monthly we complete a vacation rental lodging tax form. Quarterly we file with the state. Annually we buy a rental license and file federal taxes. All these forms are supplied by the agency's wanting them.

The forms we use are very simple, mostly homemade and designed to make sure we don't forget or overlook certain details.

Our vacation rental business is a good example and a major part of our landlord business. The form we use most often is a 2" x 4" self adhesive mailing address label. We print the labels thirty to a sheet and pull one off each time we rent a date. We adhere the label to the front of our rental agreement. On the label I have listed all the steps we take when renting a property. For instance #1 is the date, #2 is $ amount, #3 is update calendar #4 is e-mail confirm, and so forth. We check off these important steps as we complete them. If we get interrupted by the phone or go to lunch, our checklist label reminds us where we left off. The last item on our list is the deposit refund and then we close the notebook. Our next most used form is our rental agreement. Again, I create this form in the computer and print out copies as needed when I rent vacation rentals. Anyone could easily create our custom forms or your own. Our rental agreement looks professional. I created borders and set margins, I chose fonts and sizes and I print it on 8 ½ x 11 paper so it fits nicely in a three ring binder. It is not something special that needs to be purchased, it is simply a reminder list of information I want for my records. Names, dates, address, phone numbers, arrival date, departure date, vehicle info. The bottom of the form includes our refund policy and house rules. We have changed our form (updated) many times over the years. Our first form was based on something I found in a stationary store that listed a massive amount of useless (to us) items. I cherry picked items and typed my own custom form. As our needs change I change the form. For instance a while back I updated our free cancellation policy from 30 days to 60 days. Very simple.

Our month to month (as opposed to our vacation rentals that we keep in a notebook) rental information is kept in two file folders we have for each home. One folder is for house information like original closing papers, taxes, bills, insurance policy's, remodel and repair info, perhaps some paint chips and color formulas, appliance descriptions and serial numbers, and a stack of warranty sheets that get purged decades after expiring. The other folder is for tenant information. Each new tenants papers are placed in front of the last. I keep the old ones forever or until I run out of room but in reality don't need to.

For tenant information, I collect personal and employment references. I save information about their prior landlords and addresses. I keep a signed copy of our rental agreement. Our month to month and lease agreements are variations of off the shelf ones I bought thirty five years ago.

Primarily our agreement documents money exchanged and what we both agree to do. Recently I updated my agreement to say I will charge their deposit and last months rent deposit for expenses they incur that they have not paid. An old water bill or trash service bill is an example.

By now you have read me say repeatedly to do your own thinking and not be a lazy thinker. This book is about what I do, not what you should do. My hope is that readers will benefit from our experiences and then chart their own course making their own rental owner future better.

About collecting information. I write down and save in my files tenant phone numbers and addresses I become aware of over the years. Mothers, brothers, in laws, etc. I also record check information such as banks and credit unions. If a tenant always sends me money orders and then one time sends me a credit union check or strange check I record the data.   Hopefully you will never need to dig out information but we have needed to and it may be helpful for you too. So why not write it down when you can. Case in point. One time we garnished a checking account for bad checks a person gave to us. The amount was several thousand dollars. We were unable to collect because their account always had insufficient funds. I went through my records and discovered one time he had written a single check on a different account from an out of town bank. I delivered the garnishment order to that institution and received payment the same day. The person was hiding his money but I found it because I had saved the bank name. Today I write bank names and other useless notes on the back of our rental agreements. $2,500 made me a believer.

When tenants give notice

Sometimes receiving a, "I'm moving phone call or note," comes as a surprise, sometimes it is welcomed. If I don't know why they are moving, I ask. Several times I have lowered the rent allowing the tenant to stay longer, but invariably they move. If I can stretch it out I can work repairs and maintenance into my schedule. More importantly it gives me more time to find a new tenant, and time for that tenant to give notice.

New tenant, current tenant, new and past landlords are all tied together today. The more notice we all have, the easier it is for all of us to get the job done and make money.

Maintaining a cordial relationship with an outgoing tenant pays dividends. Today tenants value landlord reviews and so are more willing to work with disruptive showings and repairs.

When landlords give notice

We have given notice to move a number of times, usually with bad results. The easiest to believe excuse is telling them you want to do a big remodel, or sell the property. Giving six months notice and then being flexible helps, but the outgoing tenant has no real reason to be nice or reasonable, especially if you start pushing.

On a few occasions we wanted to raise the rent substantially. I did not want to lose my tenant or be a mean uncaring landlord, what to do? I talked with them, asked them what they could afford and offered a slow transition to ramp up the rent or take their time moving.

We have sold houses with the tenant. As you can imagine showing a place for sale around a tenant and their mess is about as unattractive as you can get. Our feedback from buyers and agents is generally negative. Consequentially we have had few offers and low offers.

One time a buyer called me after walking through an **176**   occupied house. He asked if I had seen the inside. I admitted I had not been in the house in many years. He said it was in bad shape and the tenant was being a real jerk. He also said he wanted to buy it as is. We made a private contract deal and I would assist with evicting the tenant if it came to that.

I think that open and frank discussion is important in day to day dealings with tenants. But when a landlord gives notice to vacate, I think it is critical to give notice in writing following your local laws. You should still talk, but prepare for the tenant to turn and fight. The system is becoming punitive and anti landlord with mandatory fines. We have never been fined but one time some militant young tenants went after us for perceived structure violations. Fortunately we were in the process of wrapping up the sale of the property. The new owner took title and all the problems including the unfriendly renters.

As a side note, the above mentioned renters are an example of a tenant to fear and I should have seen the red flags.

Left at the Alter

Being a landlord means making appointments to show property, to fix property, to buy and sell things, to make arrangements. I meet with all sorts of people for all sorts of reasons.

Getting stood up for a dinner date is one thing, but leaving a landlord standing on the porch is bad business and requires action. To this end I have adopted an attitude to protect myself. I believe that the less a person is involved personally, the less they can be trusted to follow through or do what they say. I call them unqualified as a catch all phrase for people that initiate contact and then dump on me.

Unqualified people begin with walk bys or drive bys. Next will be newspaper leads and yard sign callers. Today it is people that call or worse, text from craigsliist or other online freeby's. An observation of mine is that the more excited and the more times they contact me, the more unqualified they are. That seems to be the opposite of what one would expect, but I've seen it play out for years.

Even today in our vacation rental business, I get callers that want to talk and talk. Often those are the ones that don't rent and waste my time. Unqualified red flags, yes, but I don't know for sure so I take the bait everytime.

With a few exceptions, I wont agree to meet in person with someone that falls within my definition of unqualified. Of course you can't run a business this way so my solution is to make sure I have another reason to be at the property, such as some sort of minor work or picking up something. I have even brought a book to a meeting that I suspect might fall through.

This is not a problem only I have. I have had others tell me they have the same issues and how refreshing it is that I show up as arranged. It certainly seems like a no-brainer good business tactic to simply do what you say.

Take pictures

When we were acquiring property, it was hard to remember what each place looked like. One house, Linda and I couldn't remember if it had a 2nd bathroom. We learned to take lots of pictures for our files. Not only do pictures substantiate your rentals condition but they allow you to sit at home and dream up renovations.

We try as best we can to record appliance models and measurements, we also try to record paint color formulas. I say try but we don't do a good job of it.

Lock boxes

New places always need a bunch of work, probably with a number of people. On day one I install a combination lock box and attach the key to the lid with a cable tie. Now when the floor guy wants to measure he can let himself in. Same with the rest of the contractors. It is important to attach the key to the lid or it will get lost.

I avoid giving the lock box code to potential tenants. I will make an exception if I have already met with them, but not strangers.

Deadbolts versus keyed entry locks

We learned a long time ago that tenants lock themselves out. Next they break in or call you. Neither is acceptable. My solution has saved me tons of repairs and headache. I supply my houses only with deadbolts, not double cylinder, singles only. This means on the inside the tenant turns a knob to lock up when they are home. When they leave they must use a key to lock the door, no more keys locked in the house, no more phone calls or break ins.

The other lock and latch is spring loaded, that's the one that locks behind you without a key. I either replace it with a non locking one or more likely I disable the one that is there. If it is the locking type it is a simple matter to remove the shaft that connects the turn button to the cylinder.

In our neck of the woods, new tenants are required to receive new created keys, never used before. This means it is not allowed to switch deadbolts with your rental down the street or an old used deadbolt you have been saving. You must rekey or buy a new one. This rule is another good reason to buy inexpensive new deadbolts and not two set packages.

If you missed my point that's okay. In a nutshell, any entry door that may be locked by simply pulling it shut behind you is not allowed in my rentals. I require doors to be locked with a key from the outside, this way we don't have accidental lock outs. I make this change asap after getting a new house. I don't like interior doors with any kind of lock or hook latch except perhaps bathroom doors that may be unlocked with a screwdriver.

Lost treasures

Cleaning out a rental can be drudgery, it can also be a grab bag of goodies. Our kids used to love helping on the first day only when we got a house back. Especially if the last tenant had a bunch of kids and played the many charities that abound in any large city.

At first I was astounded and amazed at what the non wealthy threw away. Food, toys, clothing, electronics, furniture. I have come to the conclusion that if a person is given everything, they don't value it. I guess that is why parenting advice is to make your kids earn what you could simply buy or give them. We had to say no a lot or our home would be over run with plastic things.

Sometimes I had to quit looking at what I was throwing in the dumpster or I wouldn't get any work done. The kids, I let play and have fun, it was like a free day at the thrift store sometimes. One time I hired two laborers to help empty a three bedroom that was stuffed with everything under the sun. I told them, "don't even look at it, just toss it." Later after dark when the dumpster was getting full one laborer came to me and said, "I know you said to toss everything, but I thought you should know, I tossed all the disassembled components to a complete bicycle, I think an expensive one." I took my orders back and said dig out the pieces, I want to see it. It turned out to be a one year old Trek brand. I took it home with me and the next day called a bike shop, they said that model sells in their store for $549. It's been twenty five years and Linda still rides it. With newer tires of course. That same place scored us a water weighted $350 basketball hoop, it's still in my driveway.

Most treasures that we have way too many of are, heaters, box fans, radios, tools. It's easy to think something is cool or valuable only to realize later it is junk after all, but not that 50 gallon aquarium set up in my office or that litter of kittens we resettled.

Selling items in garage sales and online has been a way for us to recover some of our lost income. Donating to charities is how to save on dump fees and put good items to use.

Supporting tenants

I have talked about steering clear of tenant friendships, but that doesn't mean I don't support my tenants. For the most part anytime a disagreement arises, people join sides and go to battle. Smart people don't get involved, but if a neighbor calls me on the phone, what choice do I have?

Fence straddling is one answer. When the nasty neighbor calls to complain or give me a piece of advice he is in essence wanting to vent his rage over my tenants behavior. It is natural to become defensive but I listen patiently and think about how to appease him. What he wants is for me to agree with him and do something. If he is justified, it is easy to jump on board. If the neighbor is complaining about cars parked in front of his driveway or mailbox, I readily agree that he is right to be upset and tell him I will see what I can do. But I already know that he should call the city or county over parking violations not the landlord. If the neighbor is irate I try to end the conversation asap with him thinking I am taking care of his complaint.

For the neighbor it is mission accomplished, he has vented. I may or may not contact my tenant. It all depends on the rest of the story and my knowledge of the situation, the neighbor and my tenant. I have had neighbors that are absolute gems for decades that I cherish and preserve our relationship. Most of the neighbors are renters themselves, they come and go. Some neighbors are the real problem not my tenant. The action on my part is the same regardless of who is complaining. Listen and hint at but not promise action.

When I talk to my tenant, I have one goal, save the peace and dial back my involvement. In essence I am now the irate neighbor venting at my tenant, that puts my tenant on the defensive. Instead I talk about something else and make the neighbor issue more of a side topic I bring up after we chit chat. But not always, sometimes my tenant is dead wrong and a real problem all the time. I remind him or them that a condition of living in my house was that the police and neighbors don't ever call me. If appropriate, I suggest they are close to being given notice.

If my tenant is a perfect angel and I assume they are, just like my children are. I carefully broach the behavior subject and make sure I come across as 100% in their corner, (somewhat like with the irate neighbor). I lay out the neighbors issues and ask them to find a solution leaving me out of the equation. With normal adults and regular people, simple communication or lack there of is often what is going on, not a turf war.

We raised our bar so to speak by improving our property locations. Subsequently neighbor and tenant behavior improved. Problems are rare nowadays. The children grew up too.

> *Fence sitting landlord*

I think that it is natural to interact with all people according to how each party perceives the other and this includes tenant landlord relationships. This means that a tenant that thinks the landlord is their good friend and a great guy may take advantage of their friendship. For example the rent is due on the first and I expect it on the first but my good buddy renter is carefree and knows I don't mind, so he sends it to me any old time. Same thing with behavior. Lets suggest this same renter lets the grass get so tall that neighbors complain to me. I don't like any of this, I may be a great guy, but I am not their friend to abuse.

Readers may say I rented to a bad tenant and now I have a problem. I totally agree with that assessment but now what can I do. Children and renters and people in general push all the limits but most stop when they encounter resistance or push back. For example, when driving our cars and we see a police car beside the road, I think most of us check our speed and reflexively slow down. The reason we watch our behavior is because we respect the cops authority and believe he will enforce the rules. Same thing with landlords and tenants. Bad tenants behave better if they fear repercussions. Good tenants don't do bad things but even great tenants might think late rent is acceptable because they don't fear or expect a negative result.

I have laid out a common situation landlords may experience and I experience. Late rent is sure to annoy any landlord and there is not much any of us can do to influence our tenants except convince them of our sincerity and willingness to follow through with painful eviction or imposing expensive late fees.

I make a point of impressing upon my new tenants, I am not to be fooled with. I admit I put on an act, my Jekyll and Hyde personality comes out. I don't go overboard and I don't perform too crazily before we have a deal but I do try to make a strong point. Usually right after signing the rental agreement while we are going over details, I will tell some stories. Relating to late rent.

Here is an example I have retold many times. I lower my voice, move closer and say "I don't worry when the rent is late, I just assume you forgot to give me notice and I am to apply your last months rent." I leave it at that, letting the new tenant draw their own conclusions or prompt me to be more specific.

That single sentence story leaves a lasting impression that I am serious about rent, and I have an automatic response when I don't get it. Much like the policeman writing a ticket.

It is difficult to intentionally be an ass, unless you really are. Some readers will think I am needlessly being an unfriendly jerk to my tenants. I must remind them (readers), we started landlording with property in the worst part of town with tenants that their entire way of life is based on making excuses for not paying bills and asking for extensions knowing full well they could not pay. Imagine a delinquent child that lies constantly and gets in trouble every time they go out. Now imagine it's your child. Tough love should come to mind.

At first we rented to anyone that had some cash. We had few applicants with jobs. Offering to pay us later was normal and a costly mistake to believe. The cliché, *cash talks*, is still my mantra. I learned to drop what I was doing and pick up rent in person any time I could. Waiting for mail or arranging to pick it up a day later was a joke on us. We all know the saying, *you snooze you lose,* how true it is.

We traded away bad neighborhoods and houses that only bad tenants will rent. I don't threaten new tenants anymore, but I am on guard, Mr Hyde is nearby or is it Dr Jekyll.

When interviewing prospective tenants today, I ask about their needs, listen to their complaints. It is surprising how much a tenant will tell you about their last landlord. They should know that saying negatives affects my decisions about them.

Once we decide to rent to a tenant I outline our objectives and what I expect of them. Eventually I make eye contact and try to give a serious tone to what is usually a jovial atmosphere. I **185** tell them I wont bother them or stalk their house, or drive by once a month. I tell them it is their place to live and let live. I tell them that besides the normal stuff, all they have to do is nothing that will cause the police or neighbors to call. I say just pay the rent and let the years go by. Sometimes I ruin whatever developing relationship or friendship they may be entertaining, but I don't want to be friends.

Prime directive is a Star Wars theme, mine is simple, pay the rent, don't call, and sure as hell don't cause the police or neighbors to call.

You snooze you lose

Cash talks

Deposits

Some of my children and their friends pay rent (not to me) and deal with managers and landlords all the time. I hear an all to familiar story, they are not getting all or sometimes any of the deposit back. I hear the tenants side of the story tempered with my own knowledge and I have come to one conclusion. I think it has become standard practice in the rental industry to grab deposits using any flimsy excuse they have. I don't believe any of the petty things I hear justify what is going on.

I give back deposits, it is morally, ethically and legally the right thing to do. If I charge my tenant for something, I don't pile on costs I will incur anyway.

186

Good intentions - dumb rules

It should come as no surprise that local and state governments regulate the rental business. New rules come out every time someone has a meeting at city hall.

Most rules make sense. Smoke and other alarms are a given. The fire marshal gets involved with the total number of occupants, so does the city. When Lincoln City annexed our area we suddenly had to apply for and be issued permits to run vacation rentals. We worried that if we were turned down due to neighbor complaints we could be forced out of business. The city also limited one of our homes to thirteen people, the other sixteen people. This move overnight slashed our income and caused us to turn away some regular church groups we had cultivated for years. This was a big deal causing us to convert one home back to month to month tenancy.

I am reluctant to pass judgement on a community policing itself. I really don't know why they do what they do and how can I not be biased.

In Portland and other city's they have made rules about rent increases and notice to vacate time restraints. I think most rules are fair enough but it is very important to be in compliance. Some rules penalize landlords over simple mistakes. Such as not telling the tenant in writing within so many days the disposition of deposits. A simple omission or missing a deadline can get costly.

All these little rules are constantly in flux, I search the Internet for up to date updates and try not to be unfair with our tenants. We have never been fined, penalized or threatened for abusing a renter.

> My Prime Directive is simple, pay the rent, don't call, and don't cause the police or neighbors to call.

187

Chapter 9

Care and Feeding

Care and feeding of renters

Renter or tenant is not a bad word. Neither is landlord but to listen to some people's comments you would think otherwise. I think the number one proper thing I do is respect renters. I believe you cannot hide your true feelings toward others. I think a disingenuous person comes across as exactly that. I know where my income comes from, I know renters are an integral part of what I do, own, and my net worth.

Once years and years ago, I was lamenting to a co-worker at a construction site. I was complaining about the woes of being a landlord and some sort of dumb problem I was having. This guy stopped me cold when he said, "At least you own a home." I had sixteen units at the time. I felt like a jerk and I shut up. Since then I have tried to be more appreciative of my good fortune and the integral part renters play in it.

Last thought from Mr Hyde, don't think for a moment I can't come down hard on a tenant that is not performing as agreed, that's not being disrespectful, that's business, the landlord business.

Care and feeding of, neighbors

I try to be friends with neighbors, after all, tenants come and go, but many times the neighbors will last for years. I limit what I share with neighbors, they will use it against you. If you off hand mention your property is dividable, the neighbor will think row houses are coming. If you mention urban blight, he will take it as a personal insult. If you mention you own other homes he will assume you are wealthy and taking advantage of low income people. I have been called racist for not staying (buying) in my own neighborhood.

Talk about fishing that's a pretty safe topic. When I work on houses, I look like any other contractor. Sometimes I will say I manage the property or say I represent the owner. Sooner or later it comes out I am the owner, then peoples attitude and comments change abruptly.

I try to find something helpful I can do for the neighbor(s), perhaps offer to haul their junk to the dump when I make a run or share a bark dust purchase. If I can befriend the neighbors maybe they will become an ally, instead of a pain. Sometimes it will backfire, the neighbor thinks we are buddies and starts calling to report little problems I already know about.

Good fences make good neighbors

This title should not need discussing if it were true. Neighbors come in all shapes and sizes and good fences don't make them suddenly become good neighbors

Story time. One neighbor told us not to step on his property during fence construction. We complied.

Another time a renter living next door to my rental said when he opened his car door it would hit the fence damaging the door, would I mind if he moved ten feet of the chicken wire fence over a foot. I said sure. Later after he moved out the new tenant argued with my new tenant that I gave them the property.

Zero clearance garages and shared driveways were common once. They would look like a single driveway located on the property line running to the back yard between two neighboring houses. At the far back would two garages sharing a common wall on the property line.

The problem is who gets to park in the driveway. When one garage falls down what holds up the other one. When one property abandons the driveway can they grow a garden in their half, then how does the other neighbor get to the garage without driving in the garden.

Fences rot, especially when a neighbor piles yard debris against it. Fences are surprisingly costly, and when asked to share buying a new one, it hurts, I like to offer all the labor in exchange for my share.

A fenced dog secure back yard will help rent a house if you allow pets. A toddler secure fenced front yard will definitely help move a tenant with little ones.

My first choice for all fences is a chain link fence. They are inexpensive and easy to install, will last a lifetime with a little touch up paint if you happen to get one that is poorly galvanized. They are hard to damage and easy to repair. Being able to see through them trades security for privacy but they can be slatted. As a landlord, I am mostly interested in long term cost, I don't think chain link can be beat.

Care and feeding of money brokers

These people are not all the same, just like realtors they can make or break a deal at worse, they can make a miserable mess of a deal at best. Not always, this is just my opinion. I have applied for more loans than I have received. I think you can recognize the bad brokers on day one. They don't have answers to simple queries or make up stupid answers you know are wrong. Brokers are just salesmen, they are selling a product. They might have one product or a dozen. They may or may not know anything about what they sell. The broker on the Internet or down the street might be selling a different dozen products with different rates, requirements and levels of exasperation on your part.

It is hard to drop a deal you suspect is not quite right, I know it is for me. Each day I continue with an outfit that is jerking me around, I think, just a little more and then it is finished, and then more problems. Many times, I would have been better off to take a hike at the first sign of un professionalism, better off time wise and financially. This is why it is so important to get the right broker at the beginning and kick to the curb the losers.

I have said this before about choices. Saying no does not mean you are quitting, it means you are shifting gears to guarantee you get up the next hill in good shape.

I have learned to size up brokers, realtors, contractors, all the people I work with. I ask brokers more than just what interest rate is offered today. Things like how long have they been at their job. How are they compensated. What other loans do they offer. Can I talk with a recent customer. If I can, I ask them if they would do business with the company again. You can find out all this information during chit chat mixed in with loan questions. I am reluctant to agree to a credit check until I have decided to move ahead. You will notice with loan brokers, credit checks are first on their list - why is that? That's right, it locks you in with them but they say it is to get you the best quote.

Care of realtors

Do you need a commission hungry realtor. Heck yes, you want everyone that might help you find or swing a deal. This means loan brokers, realtors, neighbors, contractors, everyone.

This does not mean to abuse your network of contacts, just stay in touch as needed. If you are looking for property, a realtor can send you e-mails when new listings first come up that meet your criteria. We made an offer on day one of a new listing, we offered above asking price and gave only a few hours for the seller to accept. We got the house and most people never even knew it was for sale.

Realtors have pocket listings, these may be property's that they know are available but for some reason are not officially listed. One time I worked at a customers house helping with a remodel. The next time I talked with him I inquired about his project. He said he was offered a wheelbarrow full of cash to sell out as is. He loaded his tools and left. The owner had let it be known among his network that his project was available.

There is a thin line between self promotion and becoming a nuisance, I try to keep myself in check. However, we all know that the squeaky wheel and early bird gets the grease and worm so it is a line easy to cross.

Realtors are especially easy to abuse by asking for computerized information they have ready access to. The abuse is when you request things you have no intention of doing. In other words you make them jump through hoops with no possible compensation. For example asking about a listing outside your target area because you are curious.

With non-abuse in mind, We have discovered property on our own. We then handed the sale and commission to a realtor we liked and wanted to reward. It goes without saying that you will earn favors this way. Some realtors stake out a niche they prefer ie. One million and up, or no fixers. If you don't fit their ideal, both of you are better off apart.

The problem with successful realtors

The problem is their success, how can you blame success? Easy if their success interferes with your success. We have had this happen time and again.

Don't get me wrong, I am not wishing anyone less than huge success. What I am doing is pointing out something a lot of us experience. It starts out great, you meet a new realtor and hit it off. He answers your calls or calls you back quickly. He finds houses that fit your criteria and pretty soon a sale results. It seems like he is giving you personal service as if you are the only buyer on the planet Earth.

When it is time to market a property, we give it to him to list. If we find a property on our own that we want to buy, we hand him the sale to write it up. Things are going great, we are all making money.

Then one day we call him and his assistant answers the phone. Our simple request or question is not answered right away, instead we are promised a call back. The call back comes from the assistant in a few hours and results in another question and another promise of call back.

Tomorrow comes, the morning goes, I get my call back after lunch. It's the realtor himself, or not. Apologies may or may not be offered. Do you see where this is going. I could list off more examples.

What has happened is the great service went down the tube as the realtor got more and more busy being successful. What we usually encounter is a hired associate that is not as well versed. The next commission I pass out is in jeopardy of landing with a new agent and so is my next listing. We have seen this happen several times. When I hear my assistant will call you, I hear the beginning of the end.

When our kids began buying homes, I added up the number of commissions that were passed out pretty much to any takers that wanted them. Then I thought of all their friends, all entering the home market. Lastly, think of all the insurance policies a good networking agent will write up.

To all you professionals – answer the damn phone.

Care of escrow officers

Until you have had a bad one you don't realize how lucky you have been.

Most of our closings have been relatively simple and without issue. There are a lot of papers to sign, a lot of cover your ass papers. CYA is for realtors primarily in my opinion.

It is a mistake to think that title insurance protects you or uncovers all irregularities. They search the record, but small things like county or city liens and notices are not always discovered. We have been hit with sidewalk and sewer assessments afterwards, twice nearly $10,000. One time we found out that a city nuisance letter demanding performance had been issued prior to our purchase, it came with the deal.

The title company does the math, pays out disbursements and files with the county, they do not settle arguments or get involved in disputes. One time we had an escrow officer lie to us causing grief and a few bucks. We found out later the person was a relative of the buyer.

Most of our escrow officers have had an assistant field questions and phone calls. The assistant is probably key to a good experience.

You and the buyer/seller may choose a title company you both agree to. The realtors do not make this choice, but they seem to push in a direction, probably for their own convenience.

We used the same agent for many closings, we asked for her by name. When she changed companies we followed her. The difference in fees is not great enough to shop, the difference in service is.

I call the escrow agent early in a deal and ask them what they need, and if the other party is on task. I like to establish rapport. Waiting and wondering if the process is moving along only hurts you.

You can have a signing or complimentary closing in another city or on different dates as the seller or buyer. I don't know for sure but have read that my state of Oregon does real estate closings at escrow company offices, however some states routinely do closings in an attorneys' office. I think a first timer would do themselves a favor if they asked around before (get some mentor advice) how things are normally done instead of letting everyone dictate what to do and then find out they were being jerked around. My opinion.

Sometimes a problem tenant will get into trouble with the utilities and the electric company will stop service. A brazen tenant will turn the power back on. The power is easily killed by slipping insulated sleeves on the meter tabs, it takes but ten seconds to yank the meter, pull them off and put the meter back. A crafty but problem tenant will turn the power back on and then off again, stealing power. It is easy to snip the security tag so it looks unaltered. An inspector will read the meter and pull hard on the seal to see if it is intact. When a tenant continues to steal power the utility will remove the meter, but a problem tenant will go to a construction site and steal one. When the utility gets fed up with the tenants shenanigans they will cut the wires at the pole. This stops all but the most determined and resourceful tenant.

I laid out this scenario for you to understand what is happening when you are not watching your rental twenty four hours a day. When your tenant is finally gone and you legitimately want the power back on to make repairs, the power company will charge you about $300 hook up fee and require you to get a service inspection from the city or county. This is at a minimum, it could easily open a can of worms best left closed if you have any code issues.

If a tenant plays fast and loose with the water district repeatedly turning the water back on and cutting off locks, they will remove the meter and pinch the pipe closed. This will also require the landlord pay hook up costs once life has returned to normal.

It seems the utilities hold the landlord somewhat responsible for allowing their tenants to behave poorly and I think they are probably correct. As a landlord, you should know that your tenant is living without services, I doubt he is paying rent either, toss em out before things get out of hand.

Care of Insurance

I guess I have insurance, I leave that up to Linda. Somewhere I read that becoming complacent with ongoing expenses (premiums) is an easy way to get ripped off. I really should get competing quotes. Every year certain mortgage holders demand proof of insurance and we end up faxing their demand letters to our agent and never hear from them for another year. Presumably they take care of things.

Once I was working on a rental and the gutter fell off and damaged the tenants car. Our agent said I had no coverage, he said if the wind had blown it onto her car yes, but my work was not covered. He said I needed a business contractor policy which he then sold me. I am still suspicious of that advice. He added, anyone I hired would not be covered unless they were listed as an employee. It seems to me that the industry is ignoring a chunk of business from landlords or I am getting poor advice.

We were told we should increase our individual home policy's rather than an umbrella policy, they said it was cheaper and more coverage, more wonderment on my part.

A tenant was robbed of his tools once and asked about my insurance thinking it covered him. Sorry. Ever since then I have made it a point to steer my tenants towards low cost renters insurance.

We have no umbrella policy, we have two and four million liability on our individual properties, our agent advised that this was better coverage and a better premium. I do not have much confidence in our insurance advice. I really think this is an area to pay careful attention.

Since then we have closed our construction company and the insurance. If the agent is correct we have no coverage for when I work on my rentals. I am worried and I bet those reading this are thinking of their own coverage, or lack there of.

198

Unfair bookkeeping practice

This little twist has annoyed us from the first time we did our rental tax schedules C and E. I found out that I could not list any of my work as an expense. Materials I purchased or expenses I incurred are all expenses to be deducted but my labor is not. Not $25, not .50 per hour. If I pay a helper or a contractor I can list what ever I paid them but not my own labor.

I am sure there is some logical explanation why sweat equity is not an allowable deduction. Think of it this way. If I hire you and you hire me to perform repairs at our respective rentals we can both claim 100% of the invoice, so why can't we claim ourselves? BTW, you should get advice from a tax preparer not me but I think you can deduct some mileage and some away from home meals and lodging expenses for a far away rental, but we work for free.

We hear on TV all the time about how an expense is a business deduction and that is the reason why a person does a particular action. You know, like buying lunch or an expensive car. What they are glossing over is that, one must make a profit in order for an expense to be worth deducting. If all you do is create expenses you will go broke, you need to make a profit.

Do you need a property manager?

The short answer is no. A better question is, can you afford a property manager. Some will say, can you afford not to have a property manager. As in everything there are more questions and exceptions that need to be considered. Owning a rental thousands of miles from home is problematic. Buying a vacation rental on the other side of the country will pose problems with everyday maintenance. You will need help.

To be practical, most people don't need a property management company the day they buy a rental. What we have needed on day number one, was a cleaning crew and handyman and a dumpster service followed by a painter and lawn mowing. All of which we can do ourselves

199

If you intend to make your living or augment your income as a landlord and want to maximize your return you must learn to quit spending money unnecessarily.   That means the more you can do yourself the better. Some gurus will tell you that you can and should hire everyone needed and not lift a finger. They will tell you that you are better off at your day job making those big bucks. Well, I have more experience and own more rentals than many of the rental experts and I say they are wrong. It is simply not that black and white. They have tunnel vision and don't see your or my big picture.

Of course smart landlords know when to hire and when not to.   If you are all thumbs and ruin everything you get near then make the smart call and get help. If your day job is performing surgery for fifty thousand an hour, what the heck are you doing pushing a broom.

Managing your rental business is the same as any business. You will make financial decisions all year and then you add up the results to see if you made a profit or lost money. Insurance is an expense, repairs are expenses and so is a management fee. Rent is income, do the math, what's left over is your profit.   Now add 10 to 35% of your gross rents to your expenses (property management fee) and decide if you can afford to hire a manager.

The rest of the story is that all rental situations are unique. You may be tied to your desk when an emergency arises or out of town or simply don't want to handle it this time. In all cases the situation must be dealt with. You or your property manager must make the call and that costs money impacting the bottom line.

The sad news is that your property may not make any money because it requires lots of maintenance and has too much tenant turn over. Add to that a property management fee and you have a recipe for negative cash flow. If you can afford to carry the property, you may profit eventually from increased rent or appreciation when you sell.

Our first ten homes mostly lost us money every month for about ten years. I remember back then telling myself and anyone that listened that I employed myself fixing and remodeling my own houses. I also worked for other landlords earning real cash.

The reason we have spendable cash flow today is primarily because our mortgages are low or paid off. It is simple math, our rental income exceeds our expenses.

If your plan is to hire management for everything you will probably not have any spendable cash flow unless you have very low or no mortgages or rents spike again.

Chapter 10

Maintenance

Ten minute hacks to fix anything

Not really, but lets start a list anyway.

1. Ugly paint, start by trying to wash it. Painting may not be needed. Avoid changing color for faster and better looking paint jobs.

2. Sticking doors, try some paraffin or using a protective block of wood, smack the tight jamb with a hammer.

3. Door knob hole in drywall, cover with a stick on bumper.

4. Water in basement, fix roof gutter or unplug down spout receptacle.

5. Burned counter, glue 12 x 12 tile over damage, call it a hot pad.

6. Ugly carpet, cover with throw rug.

7. Constantly tripping breaker, remove excess load or replace bad breaker.

8. Ice build up in fridge, unplug and completely defrost.

9. Wood floor damage, cover with throw rug.

10. Splintered wood, use wood glue, long screws, big clamps, fill with bondo, finish with fast dry primer/top coat.

11. Rotted wood, use long screws for rebar, fill and build up with fixall or bondo.

12. Torn or worn vinyl, try patch using liquid flooring and create a design. Try a throw rug or try a click-lok laminate floating patch.

13. Loose Formica counter, try an iron.

14. Ugly tile or plastic shower, try special paint designed for surrounds

15. Ugly lawn, fertilize and over seed.

16. Ugly yard, use bark dust. It comes in handy bags.

17. Bad miter joint, switch to square corner block or rosette or fill with caulk or create new corner out of bondo.

18. Hard sliding windows, try rubbing with paraffin or a candle or soap bar.

Mr fix-it

Electrical over loads - bad tenant descriptions of problems - fridge mistakes - drain system plugs - key issues - window latch and door alignment - stripped screws - yard pruning issues ...

My success as a landlord is directly related to my ability to fix things myself. Lets face it, some investments don't have cash flow to pay a handyman his minimum charge just to show up, let alone work all day.

If you are able to pay for help with your rentals while feeding the investment to keep afloat, that is great, if not you have no choice but to learn to do-it-yourself like I did.

First lets discuss the legal issue. In Oregon where I live and play, landlords are not allowed to do plumbing and electrical work. It is okay for us to work on our personal residence but our rental property is required to be serviced by licensed contractors for certain tasks. This includes certain handyman services as well. This means a handyman is not supposed to do work on my rentals that require a plumber or electrician.

So we have some code items that will need to be checked before you jump in. For example, is it allowed for a landlord to change a fluorescent tube, what about the ballast inside the fixture. Can you as a landlord install a ceiling fan? What about a drippy faucet or how about swapping toilets. Some of the restrictions are for safety reasons, some have other underlying logic. In any case, don't run afoul of the local officialdom, make a few phone calls first.

In one of the local jurisdictions I own property in, a building permit is required to construct an out building shed. A demolition permit is required to tear a shed down and a general contractor is required to pull the permit. The landlord is only allowed to pay the bills.

With this *fix it* essay, I was thinking of a quicky fix-it article, the problem is nothing fixable is really easy to write about and is boring but I will take a shot at it.

The way I see it, if I can do a simple repair in two hours, it is the same as getting two hours pay as a handyman. If I stop a roof leak, I just earned roofer wages. When we started out I was working full time for landlords to pay my bills raising a family. This morphed to working part time for my self and part time for landlords, further morphing to only working for myself. I have come full circle. I have become that landlord I used to work for. Today I may hire someone depending on my availability or whether I have something more fun to do. I readily admit that after all these years, I don't relish working at my homes or even thinking about them if I don't have to.

I think painting skills and a selection of tools are minimally required to be a landlord. I don't mean an airless spray set up and the ability to knock out an interior job in a morning. I mean fixing little things in an hour. Window trim, kitchen walls, patching damage, ceiling stains. Learning about fast setting muds, using bondo and fix-all are very important talents to master. I can repair caved in drywall to original strength and appearance in one fast visit using materials I have on hand. Just finding someone for the same job will take more time than my repair takes and be at least $250 plus one or two more visits to inspect and make payment. It is true, sometimes we talk about a repair job longer than the repair takes.

If I were starting out today and had no skills but an aptitude for learning I would self educate myself and here is how I would do it.

When a problem or repair required hiring a handyman or other craftsman I would tell them I want to shadow them during the job asking questions and get them to share what they know. I would hire the expert only when absolutely necessary and muddle through the learning process by myself on unimportant things. You can teach yourself just about everything. With some practice you can put out work to be proud of and the money stays in your wallet. Even if you have no intention to become a skilled pro, you still need to know what is quality and required work, or if you are being burned by the people you hire.

Tools and toys

In my opinion landlords don't need to be proficient plumbers and pipe installers, however it is very cost effective when remodeling to have some skills. Landlords do need to be able to do a simple drain clearing with snakes and plungers. They also need to be able to pop off a trap and waste line and get it back together without dripping.

Normally when new renters takes over a house the plumbing drains all work. If a problem exists it should be discovered within thirty days. This means that the tenant ought to be responsible for future blockages. That being said and understood does not mean your youngish new renter will not plug up the drains and ask the landlord to fix them. I diplomatically explain to the new renter that it is likely their responsibility and after thirty days they should handle it themselves. If I am able to fix it I will. Normally I can't determine what caused the blockage and it easily could be long term issues that are not the fault of the new tenant.

Again, more expenses, the cost of a drain cleaner pro is at a minimum $75 and up and requires phone calls and setting appointments. Sometimes the time involved is worse than the money.

Another everyday fix-it issue requires a locksmith. Unless you can change a lock and adjust a latch you will be out $150 for what could be a five minute job every time you change tenants. In Oregon we must supply new keys to new tenants, so I end up with a lot of useless old lock sets.

I picked these examples because they are representative of the small jobs landlords face all the time. Don't think for a second that replacing dishwashers and garbage disposals are not common too. Right before replacing rotten stairs, decks and pruning forty foot cherry trees. Did I leave out grinding flat the raised sidewalk that the city cited me for?

My plumbing box has lots of miscellaneous gaskets and washers, an assortment of glues, adhesives, sealers and little parts I hate to toss out. It also harbors a valve seat dresser, a glue syringe, magnets, mirrors, hair snake, glazing points, putty knives, razor knives, string, self fusing tape, and a little one ounce bottle of white appliance epoxy.

My electrical box is a fishing tackle box with lots of little compartments. Inside are insulated screwdrivers, strippers, crimper, side cutters, needle nose pliers, ohm meter, flash light, wire nuts, several rolls of tape, bits of wire, one outlet, one switch and a whole bunch of little screws and small parts saved from electrical jobs.

My drill box has two rechargeable batteries, charger, a complete set of bits up to 1/2", and a large selection of drivers from star to sockets to nut. I keep several multi-way screwdrivers and a tape measure in my drill box.

I have a section in my shed where I stack my drywall and painting tools, When I plan to do wall work I will fill a couple of milk crates with tape, hot mud, broad knives, sand screens, saws, mud tray, tarps. I always bring a milk crate because I can dump it out and use it as a stool.

When I worked for other landlords, I carried all my tools all the time in a pick up with a custom canopy I designed and built. For the last decade or so I hardly have any repair calls at all. If I do take any tools with me it will only be my drill box and a screwdriver, unless I have a specific repair in mind.

Things have been very stable for us for quite a while. I think our last vacancy was over eight years ago, but when things break or need to be done I'm still the one on duty.

In the last three years or so, I switched out a gas water heater, it took three hours including shopping. I pulled the pins on a front door and adjusted the brass weather stripping, forty five minutes. I spread gravel, two hours. I painted a porch, half hour, I repaired a drywall hole, 1 hour. I did some pruning. I rebuilt two toilets, one hour each. I replaced damaged rollers on a shower door. As you can see from my list, I don't do much. *Honestly, I wish to do less.*

Repairing kicked in doors fast

First, I understand that I can't make it perfect and some homes don't require perfection, they just need acceptable and quick.

When a door is forced, nine times out of ten the jamb splinters but the door survives. Door first; entrance doors are normally 1 3/4" thick and solid core, forcing the latch side ways will split the door like a piece of kindling. Once the latch gives way the splitting ceases. I remove the knob and latch and try to squeeze the door together. If the gap does not close cleanly I look for misaligned splinters and using wire hooks and screwdrivers try to line up the slivers. I use a wood workers clamp to apply moderate pressure. If I can't get it to close properly, I will carefully pry the damaged area apart looking for the culprit sliver. As a last resort I will remove material that is holding it open. I try to reinsert all splinters where they belong if possible. Once I get it to close, I squirt the damaged area full of waterproof woodworkers glue. I hold it shut with clamps and masking tape. Duct tape leaves adhesive residue but I use it for its great strength some times.

If I am working at the house all day I will leave it to dry for at least an hour, cold weather may take much longer. If I am in a hurry I will replace the clamps with 1 1/2" screws or bring out the heat gun. I use the gold screws that look like long drywall screws. Warning; these screws have tapered shanks under the head and will split your work if you don't use counter sinks. Next after the clamps are removed I rough shape it with files, rasps and sand paper.

Seldom does a glued splintered repair come out smooth and without voids. Years ago I used fast setting fiberglass boat filler called kitty hair because I was familiar with it. One day a building inspector suggested I try Bondo autobody filler, I did and immediately became a fan. Since then Bondo and others have come out with general purpose filler that is non sagging. Great stuff. I trowel it on using putty knives and sometimes tape a mold board along the edge where the wood is totally missing creating a new clean edge. I over fill it and over catalyze the mix so it goes off in one minute. In five minutes I am rasping and sanding my final shape. A dab or two more Bondo and it is ready to paint with fast dry oil paint. Total time under one hour.

Repairing doors #2

Jambs splinter much more than doors do, the latch rips them apart, sometimes splitting the wood all the way to the top or down to the sill. The repair is the same, I align the pieces using a hook and putty knife. I use big clamps to pull it together. I try to align splinters and hold everything together with three inch screws, wood glue and clamps.

If I am missing a large chunk of wood I will use a number of long screws leaving them exposed but beneath the missing finished surface the same way rebar is buried in concrete. I then trowel on the filler using wood slats as forms. A course rasp or file is the perfect shaping tool. I almost always use multiple filler layers on severe damage repairs building up in layers. Paint it up and put the lock back and I'm good to go home in under two hours. Total cost $5 or $10, compare that to $200 to $400 in materials one or two days or worse with a special order door and jamb.

If you own a rental in a problem area with multiple break ins you must learn how to make this type of repair or you will go broke buying new doors and jambs. If your handyman can't do this he should learn. Rotten window sills and rotten sashes are seldom 100% rotted. Many are easy fixes without having to buy new. Old double hungs will rot on the bottom, I run them through the table saw cutting back to solid wood and then using glue and screws add a nice piece of cvg. For rotten sills I tear off rot using a chisel or even a claw hammer. I take it back to solid wood and then place long 3"-5" screws in a row or double row leaving them exposed but under the expected final surface. (Like rebar again)

Mix up filler, rasp, file, sand and paint. $500 saved and it is quick. The uses for Bondo filler are varied, stripped screw holes can be fixed and drilled like new, damaged counter self edges can be created and then painted. I think of it as industrial quick setting spackle.

Fixing stripped screws.

This little trick is old as the hills and something everyone should learn whether landlord or not. When a heavy door hinge or cabinet door is hanging askew and the screws refuse to tighten it is because the little screws have chewed up the wood or particle board. Lots of people simply poke in a bigger screw but fixing the original screw looks better. The secret is to fill the screw hole with something that the screw threads will grip. Often this on the spot repair is done with what ever is at hand. A splintered pop sickle stick, wooden match. The last one I fixed, I took a piece of cedar shim and whittled it to a tapered plug about 5/16" and pounded it into the damaged screw hole, I smashed it flat and scraped it flush with the hammer claws. Looks didn't matter the hinge covered it. I predrilled a new hole in the center of my plug and carefully tightened the old screw being careful not to strip it again. Once or twice I have beat pencils into oversize holes. If I ever need to move a screw hole sideways a little bit, I use this trick. Sometimes I will squirt some wood glue into the creation for good measure. Wood filler or putty works poorly, it doesn't hold screws any better than particle board and takes a week or more to harden after first shrinking.

Typical new tenant problems

I always expect brand new tenants to have minor problems. Some brought on by my overlooking something, some self inflicted by the tenant. New tenants tend to notice and want all the original trappings the house was built with. Chances are you as the landlord gave up and tossed out the ratty window screens damaged by years of children. The new tenant wants them back. You ignored the loose brick, the new tenant wants it noted as prior damage. If the yard has solar lights left over from a ill advised illumination attempt, better remove them.

New tenants seem to find long forgotten issues, some want them fixed, some don't want to be blamed.
- Gfi outlets are culprits.
- As are slow drains and faucet drips.
- Breakers that trip with hair dryers or powerful microwaves.
- Accidental lock outs
- Fence boards loose and gates that don't unlatch from one side
- Gutters that drip.
- Tenants not familiar with disposals and dishwashers need help
- Parking problems

I ask tenants to make a list and let me know in the first month after moving in. Drains commonly get plugged between tenants. The new tenant can't be blamed for preexisting problems, and the old tenant is gone. I didn't do it, why should I pay but I do. I tell new tenants that after thirty days, any stoppages are their problem to solve. This strategy can back fire because the tenant will be looking for slow drains and then I end up clearing a non problem. Some drains always flow slower than others just like some rivers.

A problem with all tenants is communication. Sometimes they are simply telling you a FYI but it comes across as a complaint demanding your attention. A frustrating problem is when the tenant is unable to clearly explain something they want fixed or changed. I prefer to make a house call prepared to fix or install something in one visit, but if the tenant says confusing or contradictory descriptions on the phone or e-mail, I have no choice but to first go figure out in person exactly what the issues are.

Recently a single mom tenant left a confusing voice mail, it went like this. "I still want to live in the house, I had some family fix the holes in the walls." I don't know what she was talking about. I am making an exploratory house call visit today.

Tile versus marble versus laminate

Don't let my petty peeves dissuade anyone from glitzing up your rental like Las Vegas or a cruise ship. It's your money, spend it and have a good time. Make your rentals something you are proud of. It is way too easy to become so obsessed with penney pinching landlording that you don't do or create things you like just for the fun of it.

For me, I know certain things in homes are wear items and for some reason rental homes seem to wear more than owner occupied homes. Many times Linda and I have commented on how the paint at our home lasts and lasts but the same paint in our rentals is washed down and painted over innumerable times. Usually during the discussion I mention that with our seven kids we have never had to clean taco sauce from our ceiling or repair fist size holes in the walls. Things that are all too common when we get a house back and not limited to low rent homes.

All floors, all counters and all walls are wear items, ceilings get a pass most of the time except for infrequent smoke and grease damage. Light fixtures are wear items. Wear items cost our bottom line, both materials and labor and impact our decisions.

I used to install commercial grade vinyl in kitchens before laminates like Pergo were developed. Now I prefer the laminates, however after doing half a dozen or so floor installs it has become painfully apparent that there are some inferior products at the stores that are simply not worth putting down no matter how cheap they are to purchase. If price and time are my only issues, I will choose carpet for large areas and plan on repeating the job. (no carpet in kitchens and bathrooms for sanitation reasons)

I love tile and granite, the look certainly adds value but a single accident can break stone or ceramic ruining a counter. That accident may happen the day you finish while cleaning up. A cracked tile in the

212

middle of an entry floor, may or may not require fixing but it is noticeable most of the time. It is true vinyl and laminate products may be scratched and carpet stained but seldom does damage bring the house crashing down sending renters screaming into the street. Some laminate flooring is darn near impossible to scratch and is idiot proof to install. Thumbs up for me.

The former paragraphs were all landlord speak, If I'm prepping for an eventual sale, I will choose stone and ceramic for tasteful touches. For an entry that is only thirty square feet I will go for the best and most impressive, the price on a small area is well worth the impact.

Chapter 11

Special Issues

Section eight is no good

Baloney, I just had to get that out. I have heard lots of ignorant wannabe's tell me all about the horrors of section eight, pure hogwash.

HUD doles out money to county's to assist certain people they have determined need help. The county runs the program with HUDS oversight. Elderly, disabled and single parents with children are the ones we have dealt with. Single female parents being the most common.

Because this is assistance it goes without saying that the tenants will be low income, this means low income parts or town but not always. We have had section eight tenants in some pretty nice neighborhoods and homes. The neighbors and schools have no clue. As it should be.

In a typical section eight phone conversation the applicant will ask at the beginning if you accept section eight. If you say no, end of conversation. Because most landlords say no is the reason the tenant asks before they ask about anything else. From a tenants standpoint it must be frustrating being constantly turned away like you were a poor person.

In most situations the tenant is pre approved for a certain amount of rent and number of bedrooms. Your house is then inspected by a county section eight person. They will look for dangerous situations, ie. loose railing, broken windows and determine fair market value, or in other words how much rent they will pay maximum for your house with that tenant. Once you fix the houses flaws and re inspect they retroactively start the rent beginning back on day one. You may end up waiting two months before you see any checks, then they catch up and flow like clockwork.

Most rent agreements will have the tenant pay some rent and section eight pay the rest, sometimes 95/5, sometimes 5/95 or even 100%. If the tenant works and gets a raise they will increase their share.

More Section 8

Our experience has been that fair market value rent as determined by section eight is usually a little higher than normal. For example a house we would rent for $1,195 will bring $1,230 on section eight. Three and four bedroom homes are gold on section eight, and having a one year government lease is nice too.

You can request yearly rent increases of about 3% or not renew and get another tenant, even a new section eight tenant. The program requires re inspecting the house annually at renewal in case it has fallen down.

For a period of time we had ten homes all on section eight, it was really nice getting that one big check that would not bounce. If the first fell on a weekend or holiday the rent check came the Friday before.

The program is rife with fraud and abuse, most which doesn't affect landlords. It is common for a single mom with kids to have a man living with them, sometimes the children's father. Many times a section eight home will have lots of ner do wells living there, all of which is against the rules. It is not the landlords job to police the system.

I remember a young girl tell me she was going to get pregnant so she would qualify for three bedrooms instead of two. Section eight is a way of life for generations. There is more incentive to stay poor than to excel.

A house we have today in a middle class neighborhood has a section eight tenant that works as a paralegal. She failed an annual inspection when they caught her mother living in the garage. On re inspection they passed, the house passed and my checks still arrive in the mail.

Without a doubt our experience has been positive and with less vacancies with the section eight program, however it is somewhat of a pain to get started each time with a new tenant.

Absolutely not

Absolutely not, when I interview prospective tenants, it will seem like a casual conversation, but I am sizing them up. I look for red flags. I don't want scary tenants, or one that will turn me in for some concocted violation.

I look for green flags too. A capable tenant that can fix little things means she won't be calling unless it is really serious. A tenant with capable extended family is another green flag. Complainers and scaredy cats are a red flag. They will complain about the house, a red flag for sure. We have all heard about the person that is so afraid of a mouse they will hide in their car or climb a ladder. Come on be honest, what will they do when they see a line of ants heading for the dog dish.

You can carry this attitude too far. A tenant that finds small problems acceptable may not tell you when a real serious issue comes up. Once we had an up down duplex and the lower unit had a pipe freeze that began leaking. It was a small leak, but it flooded the storage basement up to the level of the first step and then ran under the door into the street. When I found out, the tenant said it was that way for a week, but they didn't care because they never went down there. I cared, I cared a lot, I paid the water bill and my property was suffering.

It's certainly okay to pass on an applicant, you will never know what you are missing. It is equally important to interview the family, I may like the parents, but recognize the teenager as big trouble. Don't kid yourself, you are renting to all of them, including their friends. We haven't even mentioned pets.

You won't find any of this insightful information on the pages of an application. You must talk to them, dig a little, and in my opinion, come away with a gut feeling.

What is normal?

While writing this book I have discussed with my family aspects of landlording. It should come as no surprise that we disagree on things.

Apparently opinions run in my household.

Linda recently said about my stand on triple net agreements that she would never rent from me. My demands were unacceptable, I snapped back that she was not my target tenant and I would rent to someone else. "Fine, you do that." "Fine."

My son stopped by and mentioned his tenant wanted him to replace the broken dishwasher. He had been on the way over to the property to check it out when the tenant called back saying never mind, her daughter showed her she had pushed the wrong buttons. I remember my son telling me this same tenant having little to do lists for him when she moved in. I predict she is not done and even though she is a nice likable person, my son will become the first person she calls when the light bulbs need changing.

I suggested he could require his tenants to be responsible for certain things, just like a commercial lease. In exchange the rent is reduced. In another chapter I told of how I quit supplying appliances in certain houses and how we had no trouble finding willing tenants.

My efforts for many years and especially lately has been to get tenants to leave me alone and pay the rent.

Right after saying she wouldn't rent from me, Linda said , that's not the way it is normally done." That is the statement I want to highlight, *normally done,* who cares what is normal? What I care about is running my business efficiently, and if that means inventing new ways to do things. *Fine.* Just my opinion.

It is true that some parts of town have their own pricing. We all know of certain gas stations that are always cheaper or more expensive. And the supermarket that takes foods stamps enticing low income shoppers. Did you know that some of the big stores raise prices in low income areas? A fiend of ours that manages a chain store told us that they have five pricing areas in Portland and the highest prices were in areas the people could least afford it.

When I interview potential tenants, I ask them where they are from but I try not to openly interrogate them. I want to know why they want to move into the neighborhood. If they say they can't afford where they want to be, I see a huge red flag. I know they will be unhappy and move along as soon as they can. This is one reason for using for rent signs in the yard, they target tenants from the area.

I am skeptical of people that call from my ads where the caller has no idea where my property is or the names of the main roads. It means they are shopping price outside their preferred comfort zone.

I don't get excited when they call wanting to see the inside when they haven't driven by. I say first they must drive by or better yet when I am there but I usually wont make an appointment unless I have more people lined up or some work planned. I don't tell them I am not taking them seriously, but I am not. There have been times when I am working in an empty rental expecting a prospective tenant and I see a car slow down, obviously checking out the house but they keep on going, standing me up. After a few no shows I learned to protect my self from time wasters but it is still irritating when it happens.

While we are on the subject, you would think that when a renter calls and the first thing they say is "how much to move in." Would be a red flag, but not necessarily, in our paycheck to paycheck world it's normal to ask how much.

To pet or not to pet

I am amazed how many people have dogs, more so, how many that don't have time for them and lock them in the house or yard.

Our 99th home has attracted a colorful bunch of tenants in the thirty plus years we have owned it. We had this couple that at first impressed me because the water heater gave up a month or so into their tenancy and the tenant swapped it for a new one without any hassle. I think I gave him fifty bucks for his trouble. A month or so later they moved out without telling me but the rent kept coming for awhile so I didn't know they were gone.

Often my first clue that something is amiss is missed rent. When my calls went unreturned I showed up at the door but there were no humans home. Instead of humans the little seven hundred square foot house was full of puppies. There were a dozen or so Shar pei's, all wrinkly with black and blue tongues. Somewhere in the writhing mob was a mother, maybe two. The place wreaked of urine and feces the dogs were wretched. Calling it gross is too kind. It was a stomach churner.

My so called impressive tenants were real dirt bags, they were using the house as a kennel, they didn't live there. Honestly we have had better drug dealers than those two.

We cleaned up the house but could not get rid of the stench. I ended up renting it to a guy with a nose problem. He claimed he could not smell a thing and liked the house. I kept the rent low, he stayed there for eight years. Which was about how long it took for me to cool off and the smell to go away. The nice family that lives there now has no idea of the Shar pei incident.

More pet talk

There seems to be two kinds of tenant, those that admit they have a dog(s) and tell you beforehand, and those that keep quiet. The ones that are up front offer to pay a fee and are good bets to rent to. The other ones, you don't know who they are because they keep quiet.

My mistakes have always been not getting extra pet rent or damage deposit. Worse yet, when I discover later that they had a dog all along or acquired one, I still didn't demand a deposit or rent bump. It was stupid on my part when I think about it now. The tenant that deceives you from the beginning is not likely to suddenly become a stellar responsible citizen. It is likely they will have more surprises lined up for you.

When we started, our deposits were $250, today they are $1,250 -$1,500. If they offer or ask to pay (yes some offer) a pet deposit, I ask for another $350. In my opinion all pets damage or leave behind evidence of their living in the house. I don't think it can be avoided. My thinking is that with people there is normal wear and tear that is expected, with animals, same thing so you are justified in getting extra rent.

I also think that a tenant that is up front about pets will be responsible, however, pet owners seem to have a higher threshold for damage to lawns, interior moldings and carpeting. My adult children with dogs all have damage in their homes, they make lame excuses like, "it's still a puppy." We tried not allowing dogs in our vacation rentals for five years, after changing our policy to allow dogs we saw a 30% or more increase in rents overnight. I think it is almost pointless to not allow pets in month to month rentals because they bring them in anyway.

Deposits never seem to be adequate to pay for damage and of course you can charge them for any shortage, although we have never been successful in collecting. I think the real benefit to having a deposit is that some tenants want it back and try their best to earn it.

Tenants are not friends

We all have heard, never sell or buy a car from a friend. I think one reason for the rule is because when the car breaks, the friendship suffers. The same goes for rentals, you could say, never rent to family or friends because when issues arise, and they will, the relationship suffers.

Okay, so if we all agree, we must also agree never to become friends with a tenant for all the same reasons. I have thought about asking tenants to join us at barbecues, go for boat rides or have a beer. Every time I do, I catch myself and stop short. I keep my tenants at arms length, strictly business. That doesn't mean I don't ask them about their family's and show genuine interest in them as people.

Sometimes when I first meet a tenant I sense I need to make sure they understand we are not buddies. I tell them seriously, I am not their bank, I have my mortgage to pay and I am sure as hell not adopting them.

Arrogant tenants

I said earlier that I listen to my gut and must like a prospective tenant before I will rent to them. I also stay clear of people that scare me or Linda. Think about it, if a person is comfortable being frightening or angry when you first meet, just imagine how they could be when they are upset with you or their life. Now picture them drunk or high.

That being said, tenants fall out of favor at their own risk. I currently have a family in a home that the father has repeatedly acted arrogant to me. One time when he was late paying he said I had no choice but to wait because I couldn't rent the house anyway in the down market. When I heard that I thought, BS I'm the owner and would let the house sit empty. Fortunately they paid the rent before I could shoot myself in the foot and toss them.

The damage is done, I don't like him and will not cut him any slack in the future. Where is my compassion? I'll save it for someone
222   I like.

Chapter 12

Dreaded Inspections

Pest and rot inspections

Pretty much all old houses have rot and bugs and mice. Those that say they don't, simply aren't looking or can't see everything. Many mortgages for homes past a certain age require these inspections. When problems are discovered a loan may be denied or mitigation required. Sometimes money is set aside to make repairs, some repairs may be required before the loan process moves ahead.

I have been involved in two situations I will describe. At the time I was doing general rental repair and home maintenance I was contacted by a realtor on behalf of a home seller to make dry rot repairs, replacing a foundation mud sill that an inspector had identified. The repairs amounted to $6,500. The home seller did not have much money and was depending on completion of the sale. I completed the work and was paid in full. Later I found out the sale fell through. I remember at the time thinking it was a bad idea for the seller to go out on a limb like they did. I don't know what/where or from whom they took advice. My advice would have been to escrow the money out of sale proceeds and make the repairs after closing, but who asks the contractor.

My next little story involves a house I was refinancing that I had owned for a few years. I needed the cash to buy something, I don't remember what, but I called my regular mortgage broker and told him my plans and how much I wanted. He had all my finances and property in his computer and gave me an immediate thumbs up.

Later my broker said, because the house is old the new lender is requiring a pest and rot inspection. My original lender did not. I told my money guy that the house will fail any inspection. I knew of large rot areas and had been chasing wood eating ants with cans of raid.

My broker said, that's fine, he had an inspector that for $150 cash would write a satisfactory report and not get out of his car.

We finished the refi and I had my cash a short time later. Eventually I dug out the rot and killed the ants but that's not the story here.

I see rats

I believe that rats are part of society and their presence often gets blamed on landlords. If your screaming right now that you don't have rats, I will wager that you simply don't see them. Nice tidy garbage collection, high rises, lots of concrete tend to force vermin into other areas. Landscaping islands, ivy swaths, tight ground cover all harbor rodents.

The sewer systems are full of rats, empty sewer pipes are tubular highways for rats to travel around the neighborhood. I say empty because sewer pipes drain water away, they are mostly empty all the time. When a sewer line is used, for instance when your dishwasher runs, the pipe has just a trickle of food bearing water. It's like a underground lunch buffet on a endless conveyer.

Now that I have painted a disgusting hopeless picture, all is not lost. Maintaining a clean rubbish collection area is crucial to keeping vermin away. Simply hauling the trash can back and forth is not enough. Little bits that litter the ground around where the can sits is a feast for nightly visiting rodents. The ground or gravel must be kept clean, the can as well.

If there is an ivy bed, there are probably all sorts of critters living in it. Same for any brushy area. Rats live in dirt tunnels, so do ground squirrels. They live in crawl spaces, in the floor cavities, all snug and insulated. Rodents will live in one yard and travel to the neighbors dog dish every day for dinner. Both neighbors need to step up their game.

As a landlord, I educate my tenants, but I can't pick up their dog dish or yard landmine's fido leaves behind. It is frustrating to be blamed for my house having rats when the entire neighborhood is a breeding ground and the residents are unknowing zoo keepers.

I do not spread poison, there is too much chance of inadvertently hurting pets and children. If a troublesome neighbor gets wind of vermin issues and poison, duck and cover.

Sewer repair

One of our homes had a hole in the yard, a big one about the size of the lid off a tuna can. It was near the foundation in the front of the house. In between tenants while working on the house I would shove rocks and sticks and pack dirt into the hole but it always came back. Chicken wire and concrete stayed put but detours around my plugs appeared. This went on for a few years.

One day the tenant called saying the toilets were plugged up and the basement was flooding. Great, these phones calls are never welcome. I hired a rooter company and had the mainline snaked and then hydroflushed. For another $125 they ran a camera from the house out to the street.

The video showed the old clay pipe was caved in and a cavern was forming about three feet from the house, about where my troublesome hole kept reappearing. All of this was six feet below the surface.

It was obvious to me that the mainline will plug again and soon, I don't blame rats, except for opening the hole. It is simply what happens with old sewer pipe.

I got a bid from the same company that ran the snake and video, it was around $6,500 in 1990. I thought that digging a six foot hole should be less so I contacted a sewer contractor that did the job for $3,000, completing the work in one day.

I included the cost to highlight a few things. First, many emergency repair jobs, ie. plumbing, roofs, furnace, sewer, etc, result in a quick band aid and a bid for a permanent repair. Some of these emergency services companies prey on homeowners, they depend on people not getting second opinions. My second quote was only 50% the first.

Being in the fix up business my self, I know how it works. Once a contractor friend told me that he could do all his emergency work for free because of all the big jobs he landed by being the only contractor the customer talked with. My self and my friend treat our customers fairly and sleep well.

Flora and fauna and roaches

It takes all kinds of renters to make the world go. Sometimes I wish I was more picky screening, but I'm not.

I rented this house to some folks from another country and will leave it at that. Apparently they were accustomed to having bugs roaches and everything from the garden living in the house with them. They were in the house for only a few months and were unable to pay the rent causing me to make multiple visits to the property. I never go inside unless invited and never use my key except in an emergency which is never.

Trying to find someone to pay the rent I find myself driving by the property. My first drippy clue is moisture on all the windows, inside not outside. The windows are dripping wet. Water is streaming down every window on the first floor. No one is home and I am on the porch posting 72 hour notices. I peek through the window and

I see wall to wall bundles of salal laying on the floor. Fist sized rubber banded bundles are everywhere, there are no clear areas. It looks like a nursery in my house. I can see through to the dining room and kitchen, more salal and a long garden hose with sprayer hooked up to the sink.

My tenant is using the house to process this crop that they go out into the woods and pick. They then spread it out and spray it with water. They are spraying a water hose inside my house. I have had lots of people grow pot in closets or the basement but no one has ever pulled a stupid stunt like this.

FYI, I did some research, they get paid forty five cents a bundle, so there was a couple hundred dollars worth. This happened a long time ago, I don't remember evicting them, I think they may have up and left, when I went bonkers, good riddance.

So I have the house back and must put it back together. When I walk through the first time, bugs are everywhere, they are scurrying, jumping and falling from the ceiling. They are landing on my head. When I flip the bathroom light on roaches scatter, I guess they prefer darkness. I try to use the toilet to pee and suddenly can't after lifting the lid and dislodging an army. It is disgusting, I am totally grossed out and I am used to emptying trash piles of maggots, but this is inside my house. It creeps me out again writing about it.

More buggy talk

The entire main floor of the house is infested, the kitchen has lots of heavy wood drawers cabinets and bins, you don't want to read more of my description and I don't want to remember it. I worked up my list of repairs and jobs to do and left. When I climbed into my truck I was horrified I was contaminated, same thing when I got home, bugs and eggs could be in my cuffs and on my clothes.

The next day my workers showed up to begin painting and cleaning, a few minutes into it they left refusing to work until the bugs were gone.

I called an exterminator to spray death mist and it really worked great. I came back with my shop vac and brooms. There were a couple slow learners on their backs spinning slowly. Under the toilet lid was a safe zone that nearly got me again. It was a horrible gross experience.

I talked with the exterminator, he recognized my plight and knew the part of the world the renters came from. He said the conditions were acceptable to them and that they bought and stored bulk foods as a contributing factor.

I think collecting salal and spraying hoses inside made for perfect tropical bug growing conditions.

Surprisingly, the house did not suffer much, it had all VA tile floors, no carpets and was kinda bullet proof anyway. The next tenant did not have any problems either. If I remember correctly the next tenant kept his Harley in the living room because he didn't trust the neighborhood. I know what your thinking, all Harley's leak oil, but it wasn't that way, he placed a cookie sheet under it.

Inspect or not inspect

What I get to do has little to do with what I want to do. Whether I inspect determines what I have to do. I only speak for my self but I want to do very little. I don't enjoy going to someone else's house and being a handyman for free when I could be reading a book or enjoying dinner or sailing, hiking, or bicycling, or watching the Olympics or the grass grow. You may think - but it is your house. No it is not, I own it but it is a business, it's not my home.

So, if you go to inspect a rental and find crayon scribbling's on the bedroom wall, what will you do? How about you discover their unapproved dog is digging holes in the yard? While you are making a mental note/list the tenant asks if you can fix the loose gate and the garage light that flickers, the furnace that smells and the dripping faucets in three bathrooms and the kitchen. Don't forget the drafty hallway, the screen with a hole and the bedroom door that
228 squeaks.

As you can tell I am painting two sides to a typical inspection visit. One side finds tenant behavior issues, the other side brings out bona fide or not, landlord responsibilities. I listed what may be minor issues on purpose. It is my belief that if both tenant and landlord in this imaginary meeting went their own way, never meeting, they would both be better off. Weigh that against discovering a truly horrible but unlikely eviction situation.

Ignorance is bliss

So what to do is up to you. My daughter mentioned that she just finished inspecting her rental after the first six months of her new tenant. Later Linda and I discussed our daughters every six months inspection policy wondering if they (her and her husband) are fostering ill will with their new tenant or actually accomplishing anything. We heard that he was planning some work at her rental. For me, I'm writing this book in my spare time

.

More Inspection gibberish

It has been a number of years since we have had a tenant turn over (at least five to eight), but just this last month I leased a property we switched from being a vacation rental for the last eighteen years. Our new two year lease specifically states that the tenant shall take care of all maintenance including appliances. When I interviewed the tenant I verified his ability to take care of routine maintenance, he assured me his job as a hospital maintenance engineer qualified him.

So back to, *what do you do if the tenant is misbehaving,* You can demand they stop or give them thirty days notice for cause. I have been on the receiving end of a judgement where the court allowed my tenant to stay in the house after I tried to evict them. I learned that day that the judge has absolute power to write or rewrite the law into whatever he or she desires. A judge that has young children and big dogs is not going to consider crayon walls and holes in the lawn a big deal, he is going to say your rental agreement is too restrictive for normal landlord tenant relations, judgement for the tenant, next case.

So right or wrong the landlord loses anyway. I readily agree the courthouse scenario I just wrote was kind of stupid. You and I and my daughter will probably take the former action, (do nothing) the tenant will promise to be good and everyone goes home, except me, I'm not going to drive by in the first place.

Now the rest of the story, I have inspected my houses many times, but it is always under guise of something else. Checking the attic for mold, looking for leaks under sinks, or most likely the tenant has asked for a legitimate repair and while I am in the house I look around. Usually I will spot things I don't want to work on and hope the tenant doesn't care about. There is very little long term damage that is not repairable that a tenant can inflict on an older home. Think about it, floors walls counters yards are all wear items that routinely must be overhauled. I prefer to do this work in between tenants or just prior to selling. But that is just me.

Chapter 13

Vacation Rentals

One neat perk of being a landlord is that we can choose to own rental properties anywhere we want.   Of course that means we can use them ourselves. We studied online calendars of vacation rentals in Hawaii, the Oregon coast and several ski areas. The online calendars of area VR's reveal lots of info about seasonality, rents, and much more. We settled on Mt Hood, buying a dusty old home in the main residential area of Government Camp, walking distance to a major ski area.

We had instant success in renting weekends but more importantly it was a fun rental and tossed a little cash our way. We used it a lot. After a snowy season on Mt Hood we followed up a year later with two more VR homes on the coast. It has been nearly twenty years and we still own the three vacation rentals so I guess we have learned a little about how the business `works.

The vacation rental business is quite different from month to month tenancy. For starters we rent to a lot of people, but we never personally meet any of them, that's really cool. Our houses are empty most of the time because most vacationers go on weekends except July and August when one week rentals are routine.

One major difference between VR's and monthly rentals is the amount of paperwork and contacts. Each vacation visit requires e-mails and payment. We find ourselves answering e-mails daily, some days for several hours at a sitting.

We could hire a management company and step away entirely but they charge 30% of the gross rents. That would make us lose money or at least wipe out all cash flow on the house with a high mortgage.

Even though the VR's are very profitable, we have to earn it every day. We are ready to retire and have wanted to trade the beach homes for Portland homes for quite a while but the market is soft so we are considering switching to month to month so we wont have so much management involved.

The mountain home has been a big hit with our children so we are looking into making it a permanent family cabin where they share responsibility (read work load) allowing us to step back a little.

My thoughts on VR's are that they are a great investment if you also want to use it yourself but you mustn't under estimate the management involved. You get paid for your work that's true, but a jobs a job, you can get paid for doing lots of things.

VR's in general

More bedrooms and beds means more income, our VR's slept 21,22,and 24 people with lots of bunk beds. We also had two king beds in each house, and three bathrooms. This high capacity was no accident. Our large family plus friends required fifteen plus beds so it was easy to decide our niche was large groups. We looked for and bought homes to fill the bill.

We learned fast at the beach that homes allowing dogs bring in about 35% more rental dates and damage is minimal. Locations with an ocean view are requested often. Extra parking is very desirable if not a requirement for big groups. Level RV parking is asked for a lot. We also built large play structures for children and fenced the yards.

We offer the 3rd night free in the off season. You can operate without a web site using online services to secure renters. Air bnb, Vrbo, Trip Advisor, others. Craigslist leads are not good quality, we attribute this to the fact that they are mostly short notice. I don't think a VR can be successful without paying for commercial sites. We also notice that people that reserve way way in advance tend to cancel. In fact we increased our cancellation fee to make up for it. We developed a loyal repeat clientele and give them preference. Some holidays will book nine months in advance, at Mt Hood, Christmas and New

Years book years early if we allow it.

In case it hasn't occurred to you yet, you must completely furnish your homes including dishes, cable TV, etc. Hot tubs and Internet are asked for, we supply neither. Running a VR will require collecting lodging tax and filing reports, you will need a dependable cleaning person and lawn mower guy. One time our cleaning lady got a dui and was in jail leaving five guests in a row mad with a dirty house. We have done our own handyman work but that requires being able to respond quickly to emergencies which for us have been seldom.

We bought our VR's with landlording in mind not family use, most VR owners have other income and choose family first, we did not have that luxury in the beginning but now we do. Our children regularly use the cabins on their own sometimes excluding paying guests.

Maintenance has been difficult because of the time and distances involved. The beach homes are a two hour drive one way and Mt Hood is one and a half. Deferred non critical issues are piling up and emergency problems are thankfully rare.

Portable assets

When I decided to consider writing about our landlording life it never occurred to me that our vacation rental life was a completely different subject that was being ignored. After about 150 pages it dawned on me that vacation rentals are a big deal today and since we own two beach vacation rental homes and one mountain rental home for nineteen years and still counting, I should at least include a chapter or couple story's about VR's

First some history about our rental evolution. We started out buying and renting what ever we were able to acquire through sweat and providence. Of course we made some major mistakes, learned lessons and traded into better locations. One day Linda and I were particularly exasperated due to some recent criminal activity centered in one of our rental neighborhoods. I said, "Look, we don't have to own property here, we can take our assets and go anywhere we want." We decided we would not continue to rent a problem property that was vacant, we wanted it gone from our business and life. I placed for sale signs around the neighborhood and tied colorful balloons to them to make sure they were noticed. When a buyer came along I made him a fantastic deal and we were out of there.

Hawaii came up right away as a replacement. Then we rejected Hawaii because management would require local help and we needed to make a profit. Plus proceeds from our proposed rental sale would only cover about half what was needed.

We began considering beach rentals which are about a two hour drive away and central Oregon Mt Bachelor ski homes, four hours drive, and then Mt Hood, only one hour. Government Camp on Mt Hood has always been our ski area and all of us are skiers. The distance is fifty five miles. I called Vince, our regular loan broker and told him what I wanted to do and asked if he could arrange equity loans to make up the difference after we sold the problem property. He had all our property in his computer and at his fingertips. I pressured him for approximate time elements and total cash we could raise.

Armed with a shopping cart of high hopes and realistic shopping plans our next move was a family outing to Government Camp. Fortunately the late fall weather had not closed in yet so we were not hampered by snow.

Buying a second home is what most people are doing when picking up a vacation rental and so it was with us. Criteria and talk changes from, will it rent well to, which bedroom is mine. The kids chimed in with logic bending and heart melting wants. I used my proven method of rejecting deal breaker property's leaving only a few possibility's to consider. Linda and I independently chose the same house and made an all cash no inspection low ball offer.

EVEN THOUGH WE WERE WELL SEASONED LANDLORDS, WE KNEW VERY LITTLE ABOUT VACATION RENTALS AND DID NOT TRULY APPRECIATE THE MAGNITUDE OF THE BUSINESS. I hope my all caps statement got your attention. It is a mistake to think landlording and vacation rental management are the same or even a similar business. Once you remove the fact that they both use houses to generate income there is nothing comparable left. They are two different businesses. Of course like I said earlier, most people are not really getting an income rental, they are buying a second home with the intention of picking up a few bucks now and then. This dual purpose use was solidly in our thinking. Linda thought about family, I thought about income.

In another part of the book I talk about not being emotionally involved with your rentals. That is next to impossible with a vacation rental that doubles as your family's second home. Family memorabilia will be everywhere and shared with guests. Your beds, your furniture and your dishes all get shared with renters. Your tenants use your bathrooms and then you use theirs. Sound too good to be true? You don't know the half of it and thankfully never will. What you will experience is your own plate of life's little treasures.

I will talk a lot more about vacation rental specifics in the sections to come. Let me summarize where we are. We bought a ski home we all liked. Of course I had the final word but I listened to everyone. Within two years we bought two more at the beach. **235**

Today, we are coming up on twenty years of owning vacation rentals. We still own three and have thoroughly enjoyed renting to weekend guests but it has not been easy or fun all the time.

> *When you rent your second home to vacation renters, they sleep in your bed, then you sleep in theirs.*

Making money with vacation rentals

Choosing something you can rent for top dollar will require all the bells and whistles like hot tubs, big screen TV's, Internet, game rooms, leather sofas, the more stuff the better. The problem is, do you want weekend renters messing with all your expensive belongings. Furniture will get soiled and damaged, hot tubs get sick. Tenants will ruin your paddle boards and snow sleds. Of course you can lock up certain things, we did but there is a storage and practicality limit. It is easy to make rules, it is tough to enforce them, call it wishful thinking and move on to what you can control.

We went middle of the road, our first vacation rental on Mt Hood was not a castle nor was it a tiny cabin. We didn't have a lot of choices but we did reject about a dozen mountain houses for various reasons. We stayed away from painted drywall and looked for wood walls due to the moist cold conditions prevalent in vacant mountain homes. We opted for oil heat versus propane or electric for economy, dependability and kick ass performance when it is below zero outside. A fireplace or wood stove is a messy expensive needless pain for a landlord but I wanted one for me. So end of discussion. Putting chains on my tires is no fun so a level driveway very close to the main highway was a requirement as well. We knew the area well and benefited immensely from our many years skiing and hiking. The location, location, location mantra is never more true than with a mountain vacation rental or second home. Having to walk a quarter mile in a blizzard with kids and groceries because the snow plow is stuck or mia is a big issue. Don't kid yourself, storms happen and will make you wish you heeded this bit of local knowledge.

Because we are not wealthy and had dozens of mortgages, we rented the house as much as possible, even to the detriment of our family's desires. I knew this going in. It is very difficult to turn down a thousand dollar weekend so we could go to our mountain house and build a snowman.

After our first season at VR ownership on Mt Hood, we felt confident about acquiring a beach rental. Notice I didn't say second home,

237

we are in it for the money. We had learned a lot and went beach VR shopping with very specific requirements. Having a great view that could be promoted in photos was at the top. Room for sleeping twenty people was our proven target niche on Mt Hood so we stayed the course. Twenty people need lots of parking and bathrooms. We wanted an area people knew about, simply being on the coast was not good enough, the location had to be a destination location. Somewhere they would search the Internet to find. Vacationers don't want to drive to the beach after they arrive. So besides a great view, it had to be close walking distance to beach access. It had to be somewhere we could drive round trip from home in one day and still get half a days work accomplished. As a side note, we could not afford ocean front property. I think that was a mixed blessing, ocean front demands higher rent but that reduces your customer base. Parking for ocean front is very limited, many times only one or two vehicles are allowed. The other issue is tremendously increased wear on the homes exterior due to wind, and salt. We learned all this later as our homes new hedges died from salt, west facing walls became weather beaten and windows blurry from blowing sand and salt etching.

In our search for the first beach VR, we visited the cities of Astoria, Seaside, Cannon Beach, Lincoln City and all the communities south to Newport, this was the geographic limit we felt we could drive from Portland. This was where we figured most vacationers from Portland would be looking for a vacation home to rent. These were the names we found on Internet searches.

Astoria didn't have any appeal at all, we looked into Seaside's city rules on parking and number of tenants allowed and decided we did not want to deal with their restrictions. Cannon Beach is decidedly anti vacation rental and has laws keeping VR investor's out. We settled on a slightly higher priced area called Roads End, it is at the north end of Lincoln City in an unincorporated area with no rules except county and state taxes.

Lincoln City is a four hour round trip from Portland. Nowadays we only work about 4-6 hrs during each visit making a ten hour day. We do the drive about 6-10 times a year maybe less. In our early years with young children we went down for family time quite a bit. Then the kids began driving on their own leaving us at home.

Dollar for dollar vacation type rental homes cost more to buy than city rental property. They also generate more income, perhaps 100% more income. Without digging into details one would think vacation rentals are a cash cow gold mine. Now the details, as I have said before, landlording and vacation rental management are decisively different animals. Owning a month to month rental or two can and should be a passive investment, not as passive as a bar of gold but not a real job either. Owning and managing vacation rentals is a full time job and may take so much time and effort that the owner cannot run the business without hiring professionals. We now have nineteen years experience, I can say without trepidation that operating only three vacation rentals has been a year around job of about twenty hours a week during our busy season of about three months, more like two or three hours each week the other nine months Those hours worked are solely office work, taking reservations, scheduling, and house keeping management. They do not include repairs, maintenance or inspection visits.

I will give our actual numbers so you can decide if it is worth it to you. It was for us. I would have to pay 30%-35% of our gross rents to hire outside management to do what I do. That 30% is my income. The number will be different for each rental and location, ours is $25,000. Some houses do better than others, some require more time but $25k is about what I get paid each year to manage my three vacation properties. To be clear, that's 25k for three, not each. To be more clear, that is my take home pay, first the homes must pay their mortgages, taxes and operating expenses. Lest readers get the wrong impression, our rentals don't make enough to pay me a positive cash flow and a manager. If we turned our three vacation rentals over to a management company, one house would turn a profit, one would break even, and one would have negative cash flow every month. We make our money being managers, not by being owners. For our month to month rentals we make money being owners. This is a big difference, if you don't get it, you will.

I must emphasize, the real world results I just laid out are typical, if you wanted to make VR management your job, It's good pay. If you wanted to buy a second home and let vacation renters help you pay the mortgage, even better. If your plan is to make money owning VR's and hiring management - don't bet on it, but good luck anyway.

What I really do each day is up to me, I work from home, but we can work on the road with wifi hot spots. I work several quarter days in a row and then skip a bunch. I have learned what is important and what may be ignored. We spend weeks in the summer, camping or sailing and manage to run the shop as if we were at home thanks to the Internet and cell phones.

Owning vacation rentals has not been a get rich scheme for us but it has allowed us to acquire and pay down properties that we enjoy. I needed part time work for the last twenty years to complement my other part time landlord jobs, so it has worked out very well.

I remember once saying to a worker I hired or maybe it was a landlord that hired me. I said, "I am pretty damn lucky, I hire myself to work on and manage my own houses." Now, thirty five years later, I am still at it except I hire others to do the things I no longer enjoy.

Now the little secret that tells the end of our VR business. We are in the process of converting our vacation rentals back into month to month rentals or selling them on declining lease options. The reason is so we can retire and travel far away without any management duty tying us down. Financially we will take a small hit but that's what is expected when you quit your job. I wont have any e-mails to answer either.

Vacation rentals versus month to month

As a new property owner you proudly eye the condition of your rental the day you turn it over to your first tenant. Fresh paint, new flooring, it doesn't smell. Then in six months or a year later you get it back. You step in the door and you see your sad rental at its stinky worst and start over. You repeat this dance with every tenant. It's enough to bring out the inner cynic armed with a paint roller and screw gun.

A vacation rental is different, not only do you have fresh paint and spotless floors but you also have hand picked personal furnishings, wall decorations and your home reflects you and your great taste. Your first vacation tenant group of fifteen come and go and you get your home back. Upon inspection the house looks great, you may even wonder if anyone actually stayed there the last three days.

The last two paragraphs are thoughts I have actually expressed out loud a number of times. Of course over the years the VR does show wear and tear, the furniture gets soiled, cheap dining chairs become wobbly, dishes slowly disappear, so do cute nic-knacks. Overall it is remarkable how satisfying owning a VR is.

I receive friendly e-mails from tenants telling us what a great time they had and how well the house worked for them. About 15% of our guests are repeats, some for fifteen years, many come back for the same date each summer and tell me it is their family tradition. A number of guests send me family pictures. These are people I have never met but we talk on the phone and e-mail.

Not all tenant interactions are so enjoyable. We have learned that there is a type of person that complains no matter what. These complaints really do bother us and take the fun out of management to the point we are looking forward to retiring. I want to emphasize to potential VR owners that if you are bothered by negative feedback, even the so-called constructive kind (I am being kind) you may want to stay out of personal management and hire a property manager.

Here is a typical e-mail I don't appreciate. *Hi john, I want to tell you that our family had a great time at the beach but I feel I should alert you to some things about your house. The dining room window screen is torn, if it had been summer your tenants would not be able to open the window without letting flies in. There were no coffee filters. The TV does not have espn, your web site says there is wifi. (No it does not) I Can't believe you don't have a landline for family's with children, what would we do if we have an emergency? The dishwasher detergent is almost gone. The gate latch for the patio is hard to work and our dogs got out. (Our instructions say not to leave dogs on patio) We found a dirty sock under the bunk bed.....* I intentionally chose some frivolous but true issues. The point I am making is that some guests think these are a big deal and complain to us. All they accomplish is putting a cloud on a sunny day.

One last comment and then I will move on. When past guests make unsolicited comments and come across as complaining, Linda and I try to ignore the ridiculous unfounded ones but that does not always work. Some complainers demand a response and if we don't respond promptly they complain that we have not responded. My usual reply is, *thanks for letting us know.* There is no reason to continue a dialogue with certain people. Sometimes I will make notes on their rental agreement, I may write do not rent or no discounts in the future. Yes these complainers come back wanting to rent again, but I don't need them, no one does.

Vacation rentals don't attract renters. Area attractions are the draw. People go to Mt Hood in the winter to play in the snow, they rent at the beach because it's the coast. Mt hood is very seasonal, when the snow is gone and the ski areas close, so are the renters. Except for the occasional summer wedding reception our Government Camp house is only good for six short months and then mostly on weekends leaving weekdays for our family. Of course Christmas to New Years will reserve a full year in advance. Our two Lincoln City beach rentals rent year around with week long dates in July and August. Our first beach house rented 52 weekends in a row. That stellar profitable performance prompted us to buy another house one block
242 away. We have never been able to best that record.

When the bubble burst and real estate crashed in 2008, we worried that our VR income was in trouble. Rents went down and vacancy's went up significantly. We lowered our rents but people stayed home. We lost money on one house and barely made minimum wage for our time on the other. Mt hood was a cash loser as well but our family use more than justified continued ownership. We did not sell under duress, we hung on and rents came back a little each year.

I am fairly certain that few vacation rentals pay their own way plus toss off cash. Ours do but we work hard to get it. We earn our money as managers, not as owners. Anyone that says VR's are a gold mine can't do simple math or don't place a value on their time. The only real gold mine is being able to employ yourself as a property manager and maintenance man and that is only if you can use the work. I'm not saying in any way that owning VR's is not a great way to help pay for a second home, it is. Charge someone three thousand bucks to use your beach house for a week, do that math.

VR memorabilia

I can't possibly remember or list everything, but here's a few.

We have periodic neighbor issues caused by our VR renters. One time a neighbor called to complain that our guests were playing football in the street without shirts. Another time the same neighbor told us we should not rent to fraternities or Russians. One time a neighbor watched a person peeing off the second floor deck and felt we needed to know so she called us during a school conference meeting.

One of our guests bought a new Weber kettle barbeque and left it behind saying it was a gift because ours was rusty.

We have tenants forget things and want us to look for them after they have left. Many times they find their stuff at home and then say never mind. One guest e-mailed us asking if we found her glasses, our housekeeper says she found them, but I'm one hundred eighty miles, round trip.

I made an effort to bring home to Portland a special battery charger a guest left behind and asked I find. The guest lives in Portland, I called and e-mailed that I had it for him. It's still here in my office.

Kids, (I assume they are kids) would bring sand in the house and dump it on the pool table, we cleaned and vacuumed many times but we still got complaints that our pool table was crap. We removed the pool table, now no one complains.

We keep the keys to the VR's in a combination lock box mounted on the wall beside the front door of each house. We give the code to guests so that they can get the key when they arrive. One day a women called us when she arrived saying she was standing on the porch pushing the buttons but the door was not opening. Something about her choice of words made Linda realize our guest thought the door was electric and should swing open when she entered the code.

One day when I arrived for some minor task I noticed the toilet was running, I jiggled the handle and it stopped. Our next water bill was $879. No one had been at the house for 2 ½ weeks. The same thing happened a month later at our other beach house, $750 that time in one week. I installed whole house shut off valves and now require the house keeper and guests to shut off the water when vacating. So far so good, its been about ten years. We already were shutting off the water at our mountain house.

Our two beach homes are one block apart on the same street. One house collects thing guests leave behind or abandon. Towels, pillows and toys pile up. The other house is constantly missing things, we lose coffee cups, spoons and beachy knick knacks. Linda just announced to me that our daughter reported a metal shelf unit was missing from the bathroom of one house where she was spending the night. I try not to get upset when our guests steal from us, my inner cynic has learned to expect it.

One guest left black dog hair all over the bathroom and in the tub, I talked to them saying they left the house unacceptable for the next guest. She said our rental agreement did not specify they were not to wash dogs in the tub and that if I didn't return their deposit they would give us a bad review on all the web sites. I returned their deposit, what would you do?

We have had people complain that our blender wasn't any good, except we don't have a blender. Upon looking we found one in the cupboard a guest had left. On the base was the local thrift store sticker.

Sadly a four hundred pound guest broke her leg when the chain on the children's swing broke. A different guest twisted her ankle stumbling on the steps inside a beach house. It was Linda's best friend.

The coast is known for winter storms, some with hundred mile an hour winds. One storm damaged our roof to the point it had to be replaced. A series of storms eventually took out all our tall pine trees which improved our neighbors view of the ocean. Wind blown sand and salt has etched some windows ruining the ocean view. **245**

A tenant that happened to be a family friend called minutes after arriving at a house and said they couldn't find the stairway to the upstairs bedrooms. Linda told her, face the fireplace, now look to your left. I think people are so quick to grab the phone that they don't think anymore.

I have a list of instructions posted for my housekeeper to follow. One item is to go out in yard to the children's play structure and bring back kitchen dishes and utensils, be sure to check the sandbox for glasses and spoons.

The coastal electric grid is subject to salt corrosion, transformer connections are prone to failure and shorting. One morning while Linda and I were at a beach rental painting and fixing things the lights began flickering, some light bulbs popped, and two TV's started smoking. We carried one TV outside fearing it was about to burst into flames. I think we lost all the TV's, the fridge, and microwave, about $2,000 worth. The local utility company paid for all of it accepting responsibility for a short circuit in the grid. Our neighbor lost their furnace mother board. Up on Mt Hood we had a similar issue where we lost TV's when a car crashed in the snow taking out a power pole. That utility refused our claim saying it was an act of god and beyond their control. As a side note, I have never had any losses of this nature at any of our other homes.

Ever since we have had our VR's listed for sale, guests have confused realtor lock boxes for our lock boxes. The problem is no one reads or follows directions. My directions are clear. *The lock box is at eye level on the wall to right of front door*, no where do I say, *look for key box hanging from water faucet under stairs behind garbage can*. We get quite a few calls from arriving guests that can't open the realtor box.

Vacation rental daily bookkeeping 101

The following is a short and condensed version of our daily work from beginning to end when renting a beach house. This is what a property management company does to earn their 35% cut of the gross rent.

Our first contact is an e-mail inquiry that comes from a web site or Craigslist post (that reminds me, I need to renew my CL post). Craigslist often generates poor quality leads and phone calls that waste time. We get quite a few phone calls from past customers which is good but takes much longer because they want to chat. On the other hand, repeaters are easy to please.

I respond to every first time e-mail inquiry with a prepared sheet I call basic information. This is a two page document that I have saved in several formats for rapid copy and paste. Along with basic info I answer any questions and give them a detailed dollar quote for their stay. We really don't like or want telephone inquiries. In fact we consider telephone inquiries as not good quality leads, slightly better than craigslist e-mails which are real time wasters much of the time. Obviously all telephone inquiry's must be converted to e-mail. I tell phone callers that we do not rent over the phone, we have no ability to take payment, they can come to our home in Portland and pay with cash or mail us a check. Our preferred method is to e-mail them a link to pay online with plastic. Surprisingly, each year two or three people come to our door with cash.

I send out our basic info and quote to first inquiry's and forget them. Some VR managers will follow up with pressuring calls and repeat e-mails. We do no follow ups. I don't want a pressured person canceling later. We put the e-mail in an old mail folder so I can search for it later. I can complete a basic info reply in about five minutes give or take with questions. Our basic info page has multiple links to our web site where we have our calendar, photos, rate charts, detailed description and a Q&A page. It is up to the customer to make the second contact. Again, no follow ups from us.

Our second contact is hopefully not a phone call but an e-mail asking for us to reserve their date and send them the necessary rental agreement forms. It takes me another ten to twenty minutes to complete the two e-mails required. We have a prepared rental agreement that I fill in dates, amounts, taxes, names etc. This is a one page e-mail that I send back to them for completion and return with a check for payment. If they have requested credit card payment, I send them a second e-mail with links for payment online. We use PayPal for online payments, it costs us 3% that I tack onto the invoice.

After the second round of contacts, we hold the requested date pending payment. If payment does not arrive in three or four days, I will sell the date to someone else. Once again I forget them. If they follow through and mail a check or make credit card payment, I reopen their e-mails, check my notebook calendar to make sure the date is still open and finish my book work. Notice I said, *if they follow through*, about 25-35% that ask to reserve a date do not ever call or e-mail again. When they say a check is in the mail, I wait the three days my instructions say I will wait and then consider others. If I have sent them a cc invoice, I wait one day. There is no such thing as truth or loyalty in this business, money talks. We do not reserve a date without payment. We learned expensive lessons and vacant dates, so I am hard nosed. Every once in awhile a past guest will push our buttons just right, causing me to bend the rules.

You will be wrong if you sense that we are not serious about renting as many dates as we can. We have almost twenty years at this game, it does not pay to reserve a date for someone that is hurried, pressured, or not sure. Same goes for someone offering a credit card number on the first telephone contact or one year in advance. These people often end up canceling, costing us fees and hogging dates so we can't rent them. Big red flags for sure.

> *The daily rent is all we have,*
> *It's what landlording is all about*

When we get paid either via PayPal or the check arrives in the mail, I print out their rental agreement. This is the first hard copy of anything to date. We have a small (2 x 4) self adhesive address label I created with a check list of steps we must complete. I afix (funny word - afix) the label to the rental form and begin to complete the listed steps.

Date:	Final payment Ck#:
Amount:	E-mail confirm:
Ck number:	Mail Instr:
E-mail confirm:	Mark Cal:
Edit housekeeping:	Refund date:
Edit res. Cal:	Amount:
Edit notebook Cal:	Ck #:

It takes us about twenty five minutes to do the final steps listed above. The first row is done when we receive the reservation deposit. The second row is completed when final payment is received. All the rental agreements are kept in a three ring binder. We keep one year of prior seasons rental forms in the same binder so I can quickly look up repeat guests forms and any notes, plus check what we charged them. Thirty days after the rental date we send the guests deposits back to them.

That pretty much outlines what we actually do everyday. Of course there is much more to it but that is the daily work. Someone still has to pay the gas bill and make sure the garbage is collected. We have a house keeping lady that is pretty much on auto pilot. We e-mail her when issues come up. She checks the housekeeping calendar I keep updated just for her.

One might think that our busy season is in the summer, they would be half right. We rent the most dates in the summer but our heavy work is in the early spring. We book up the summer dates in February through March. By the time April rolls around our summer dates are mostly reserved. A lot of the spring dates are weekends only and we will rent them with two to three weeks notice spending only an hour each week.

We take off for vacation trips in July and August ourselves, I wonder if people even know we are gone. It is seldom that a tenant contacts or tries to contact us once they have our instructions and door key code. Our most common call is when a guest arrives and can't deal with the simplicity of our lock box. Our lock code is 56, many think it should be four digits so before they arrive, they call or e-mail asking for the rest of the code. Funny thing, if they can't reach us, they manage to figure it out anyway.

> Henry Ford said, "if you think you can or think you can't, you're right."